Practical DevOps

Harness the power of DevOps to boost your skill set
and make your IT organization perform better

Joakim Verona

BIRMINGHAM - MUMBAI

Practical DevOps

First published: February 2016

Production reference: 1100216

Published by Packt Publishing Ltd.
Livery Place
35 Livery Street
Birmingham B3 2PB, UK.

ISBN 978-1-78588-287-6

www.packtpub.com

Credits

Author
Joakim Verona

Reviewers
Per Hedman
Max Manders

Commissioning Editor
Veena Pagare

Acquisition Editor
Sonali Vernekar

Content Development Editor
Samantha Gonsalves

Technical Editor
Hussain Kanchwala

Copy Editor
Madhusudan Uchil

Project Coordinator
Sanchita Mandal

Proofreader
Safis Editing

Indexer
Hemangini Bari

Graphics
Kirk D'Penha

Production Coordinator
Shantanu N. Zagade

Cover Work
Shantanu N. Zagade

About the Author

Joakim Verona is a consultant with a specialty in Continuous Delivery and DevOps. He has worked with all aspects of systems development since 1994. He has actively contributed as the lead implementer of complex multilayered systems such as web systems, multimedia systems, and mixed software/hardware systems. His wide-ranging technical interests led him to the emerging field of DevOps in 2004, where he has stayed ever since.

Joakim completed his masters in computer science at Linköping Institute of Technology. He has also worked as a consultant in a wide range of assignments in various industries, such as banking and finance, telecom, industrial engineering, press and publishing, and game development. He is also interested in the Agile field and is a certified Scrum master, Scrum product owner, and Java professional.

I would like to thank my wife, Marie, for being an inspiration during the writing of this book. I would also like to thank all the people and companies I have worked with over the years for enabling me to work with something I enjoy!

About the Reviewers

Per Hedman is a passionate developer who is a strong proponent of DevOps and Continuous Delivery and believes that you should empower the developer and that they should take responsibility for the code that they write.

He is a software consultant by trade and has been a development and operations person since the early 2000s.

A special thanks to my wife and my two daughters for making me smile.

Max Manders is an Operations Engineer at FanDuel, the leader in online daily fantasy sports. Max previously worked in the operations center for Cloudreach, an Amazon Web Services Premier Consulting Partner. Max has put his past experiences and skills to good use in order to promote all things DevOps; he is also working to master Ruby and advocate Infrastructure as Code through Chef and Puppet.

Max is a cofounder and organizer of Whisky Web, a Scottish conference for the web development and operations community. When he's not writing code or tinkering with the latest and greatest monitoring and operations tools, Max enjoys whisky and playing jazz and funk trombone. Max lives in Edinburgh with his wife Jo and their cats Ziggy and Maggie.

www.PacktPub.com

Support files, eBooks, discount offers, and more

For support files and downloads related to your book, please visit www.PacktPub.com.

Did you know that Packt offers eBook versions of every book published, with PDF and ePub files available? You can upgrade to the eBook version at www.PacktPub.com and as a print book customer, you are entitled to a discount on the eBook copy. Get in touch with us at service@packtpub.com for more details.

At www.PacktPub.com, you can also read a collection of free technical articles, sign up for a range of free newsletters and receive exclusive discounts and offers on Packt books and eBooks.

https://www2.packtpub.com/books/subscription/packtlib

Do you need instant solutions to your IT questions? PacktLib is Packt's online digital book library. Here, you can search, access, and read Packt's entire library of books.

Why subscribe?

- Fully searchable across every book published by Packt
- Copy and paste, print, and bookmark content
- On demand and accessible via a web browser

Free access for Packt account holders

If you have an account with Packt at www.PacktPub.com, you can use this to access PacktLib today and view 9 entirely free books. Simply use your login credentials for immediate access.

Table of Contents

Preface

The field of DevOps has become popular and commonplace in recent years. It has become so pervasive that it is easy to forget that before 2008, when Patrick Debois organized the first DevOpsDays conference, hardly anyone had even heard the word.

What does DevOps, which is a portmanteau of the words "developers" and "operations", mean though, and why does it generate such tremendous excitement?

The mission of this book is to answer this seemingly simple question.

The short answer is that DevOps aims to bring different communities, such as the developer and operations communities, together to become a more efficient whole.

This is also reflected in the book. It explores many tools that are useful in DevOps work, and tools that bring people closer together are always preferred to those that create artificial borders between people. The processes we use for software development are also tools, so it is also natural to include aspects of the various Agile schools of thought as they relate to DevOps.

The book also aims, as the title suggests, to be practical.

Let's begin our journey in the land of DevOps!

What this book covers

Chapter 1, *Introduction to DevOps and Continuous Delivery*, deals with the background of DevOps and sets the scene for how DevOps fits in the wider world of Agile systems development.

Chapter 2, *A View from Orbit*, will help you understand how all the systems we use in DevOps fit together, forming a larger whole.

Chapter 3, How DevOps Affects Architecture, describes aspects of software architecture and what they mean to us while working with our DevOps glasses on.

Chapter 4, Everything is Code, explains how everything is code and you need somewhere to store it. The organization's source code management system is that place.

Chapter 5, Building the Code, explains how you need systems to build your code. They are described in this chapter.

Chapter 6, Testing the Code, shows you that if you are going to release your code early and often, you must be confident of its quality. Therefore, you need automated regression testing.

Chapter 7, Deploying the Code, shows how, when the code has been built and tested, you need to deploy it to your servers so that your customers can use the newly developed features.

Chapter 8, Monitoring the Code, covers how the code is safely deployed to your servers with the deployment solution of your choice; you need to watch over it to make sure it's running properly.

Chapter 9, Issue Tracking, looks at systems used to handle development workflows within an organization, such as issue tracking software. Such systems are an important aid when implementing Agile processes.

Chapter 10, The Internet of Things and DevOps, describes how DevOps can assist us in the emerging field of the Internet of Things.

What you need for this book

This book contains many practical examples. To work through the examples, you need a machine preferably with a GNU/Linux-based operating system, such as Fedora.

Who this book is for

This book is aimed at developers who wish to take on larger responsibilities and understand how the infrastructure that builds today's enterprises works. It is also for operations personnel who would like to better support their developers. Technical testers working with test automation are also included in the target audience.

The book is primarily a technical text with practical examples suitable for people who like to learn by implementing concrete working code. Nevertheless, the first two chapters have a less practical approach. They give you the background and overview needed to understand the motivation behind the rest of the chapters.

Conventions

In this book, you will find a number of text styles that distinguish between different kinds of information. Here are some examples of these styles and an explanation of their meaning:

Code words in text, database table names, folder names, filenames, file extensions, pathnames, dummy URLs, user input, and Twitter handles are shown as follows: "Install `git-review` on your local installation."

A block of code is set as follows:

```
private int positiveValue;
void setPositiveValue(int x){
  this.positiveValue=x;
}

int getPositiveValue(){
  return positiveValue;
}
```

Any command-line input or output is written as follows:

```
docker run -d -p 4444:4444 --name selenium-hub selenium/hub
```

New terms and **important words** are shown in bold. Words that you see on the screen, for example, in menus or dialog boxes, appear in the text like this: "We can change the state with the **Modify** button."

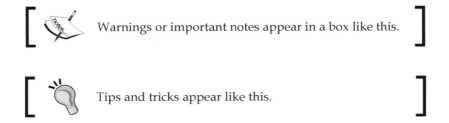

[Warnings or important notes appear in a box like this.]

[Tips and tricks appear like this.]

Reader feedback

Feedback from our readers is always welcome. Let us know what you think about this book—what you liked or disliked. Reader feedback is important for us as it helps us develop titles that you will really get the most out of.

To send us general feedback, simply e-mail feedback@packtpub.com, and mention the book's title in the subject of your message.

If there is a topic that you have expertise in and you are interested in either writing or contributing to a book, see our author guide at www.packtpub.com/authors.

Customer support

Now that you are the proud owner of a Packt book, we have a number of things to help you to get the most from your purchase.

Downloading the example code

You can download the example code files from your account at http://www.packtpub.com for all the Packt Publishing books you have purchased. If you purchased this book elsewhere, you can visit http://www.packtpub.com/support and register to have the files e-mailed directly to you.

In order to keep the code samples current in the fast-moving world of DevOps, the book's code samples are also available in this GitHub repository: https://github.com/jave/practicaldevops.git.

You can download the code files by following these steps:

1. Log in or register to our website using your e-mail address and password.
2. Hover the mouse pointer on the **SUPPORT** tab at the top.
3. Click on **Code Downloads & Errata**.
4. Enter the name of the book in the **Search** box.
5. Select the book for which you're looking to download the code files.
6. Choose from the drop-down menu where you purchased this book from.
7. Click on **Code Download**.

Once the file is downloaded, please make sure that you unzip or extract the folder using the latest version of:

- WinRAR / 7-Zip for Windows
- Zipeg / iZip / UnRarX for Mac
- 7-Zip / PeaZip for Linux

Errata

Although we have taken every care to ensure the accuracy of our content, mistakes do happen. If you find a mistake in one of our books — maybe a mistake in the text or the code — we would be grateful if you could report this to us. By doing so, you can save other readers from frustration and help us improve subsequent versions of this book. If you find any errata, please report them by visiting http://www.packtpub.com/submit-errata, selecting your book, clicking on the **Errata Submission Form** link, and entering the details of your errata. Once your errata are verified, your submission will be accepted and the errata will be uploaded to our website or added to any list of existing errata under the Errata section of that title.

To view the previously submitted errata, go to https://www.packtpub.com/books/content/support and enter the name of the book in the search field. The required information will appear under the **Errata** section.

Piracy

Piracy of copyrighted material on the Internet is an ongoing problem across all media. At Packt, we take the protection of our copyright and licenses very seriously. If you come across any illegal copies of our works in any form on the Internet, please provide us with the location address or website name immediately so that we can pursue a remedy.

Please contact us at copyright@packtpub.com with a link to the suspected pirated material.

We appreciate your help in protecting our authors and our ability to bring you valuable content.

Questions

If you have a problem with any aspect of this book, you can contact us at questions@packtpub.com, and we will do our best to address the problem.

1
Introduction to DevOps and Continuous Delivery

Welcome to *Practical DevOps*!

The first chapter of this book will deal with the background of DevOps and setting the scene for how DevOps fits into the wider world of Agile systems development.

An important part of DevOps is being able to explain to coworkers in your organization what DevOps is and what it isn't.

The faster you can get everyone aboard the DevOps train, the faster you can get to the part where you perform the actual technical implementation!

In this chapter, we will cover the following topics:

- Introducing DevOps
- How fast is fast?
- The Agile wheel of wheels
- The cargo cult Agile fallacy
- DevOps and ITIL

Introducing DevOps

DevOps is, by definition, a field that spans several disciplines. It is a field that is very practical and hands-on, but at the same time, you must understand both the technical background and the nontechnical cultural aspects. This book covers both the practical and soft skills required for a best-of-breed DevOps implementation in your organization.

The word "DevOps" is a combination of the words "development" and "operation". This wordplay already serves to give us a hint of the basic nature of the idea behind DevOps. It is a practice where collaboration between different disciplines of software development is encouraged.

The origin of the word DevOps and the early days of the DevOps movement can be tracked rather precisely: Patrick Debois is a software developer and consultant with experience in many fields within IT. He was frustrated with the divide between developers and operations personnel. He tried getting people interested in the problem at conferences, but there wasn't much interest initially.

In 2009, there was a well-received talk at the O'Reilly Velocity Conference: "10+ Deploys per Day: Dev and Ops Cooperation at Flickr." Patrick then decided to organize an event in Ghent, Belgium, called DevOpsDays. This time, there was much interest, and the conference was a success. The name "DevOpsDays" struck a chord, and the conference has become a recurring event. DevOpsDays was abbreviated to "DevOps" in conversations on Twitter and various Internet forums.

The DevOps movement has its roots in Agile software development principles. The Agile Manifesto was written in 2001 by a number of individuals wanting to improve the then current status quo of system development and find new ways of working in the software development industry. The following is an excerpt from the Agile Manifesto, the now classic text, which is available on the Web at http://agilemanifesto.org/:

> *"Individuals and interactions over processes and tools*
>
> *Working software over comprehensive documentation*
>
> *Customer collaboration over contract negotiation*
>
> *Responding to change over following a plan*
>
> *That is, while there is value in the items on the right, we value the items on the left more."*

In light of this, DevOps can be said to relate to the first principle, "Individuals and interactions over processes and tools."

This might be seen as a fairly obviously beneficial way to work—why do we even have to state this obvious fact? Well, if you have ever worked in any large organization, you will know that the opposite principle seems to be in operation instead. Walls between different parts of an organization tend to form easily, even in smaller organizations, where at first it would appear to be impossible for such walls to form.

DevOps, then, tends to emphasize that interactions between individuals are very important, and that technology might possibly assist in making these interactions happen and tear down the walls inside organizations. This might seem counterintuitive, given that the first principle favors interaction between people over tools, but my opinion is that any tool can have several effects when used. If we use the tools properly, they can facilitate all of the desired properties of an Agile workplace.

A very simple example might be the choice of systems used to report bugs. Quite often, development teams and quality assurance teams use different systems to handle tasks and bugs. This creates unnecessary friction between the teams and further separates them when they should really focus on working together instead. The operations team might, in turn, use a third system to handle requests for deployment to the organization's servers.

An engineer with a DevOps mindset, on the other hand, will immediately recognize all three systems as being workflow systems with similar properties. It should be possible for everyone in the three different teams to use the same system, perhaps tweaked to generate different views for the different roles. A further benefit would be smaller maintenance costs, since three systems are replaced by one.

Another core goal of DevOps is automation and Continuous Delivery. Simply put, automating repetitive and tedious tasks leaves more time for human interaction, where true value can be created.

How fast is fast?

The turnaround for DevOps processes must be fast. We need to consider time to market in the larger perspective, and simply stay focused on our tasks in the smaller perspective. This line of thought is also held by the Continuous Delivery movement.

As with many things Agile, many of the ideas in DevOps and Continuous Delivery are in fact different names of the same basic concepts. There really isn't any contention between the two concepts; they are two sides of the same coin.

DevOps engineers work on making enterprise processes faster, more efficient, and more reliable. Repetitive manual labor, which is error prone, is removed whenever possible.

It's easy, however, to lose track of the goal when working with DevOps implementations. Doing nothing faster is of no use to anyone. Instead, we must keep track of delivering increased business value.

For instance, increased communication between roles in the organization has clear value. Your product owners might be wondering how the development process is going and are eager to have a look. In this situation, it is useful to be able to deliver incremental improvements of code to the test environments quickly and efficiently. In the test environments, the involved stake holders, such as product owners and, of course, the quality assurance teams, can follow the progress of the development process.

Another way to look at it is this: If you ever feel yourself losing focus because of needless waiting, something is wrong with your processes or your tooling. If you find yourself watching videos of robots shooting balloons during compile time, your compile times are too long!

The same is true for teams idling while waiting for deploys and so on. This idling is, of course, even more expensive than that of a single individual.

While robot shooting practice videos are fun, software development is inspiring too! We should help focus creative potential by eliminating unnecessary overhead.

A death ray laser robot versus your team's productivity

The Agile wheel of wheels

There are several different cycles in Agile development, from the Portfolio level through to the Scrum and Kanban cycles and down to the Continuous Integration cycle. The emphasis on which cadence work happens in is a bit different depending on which Agile framework you are working with. Kanban emphasizes the 24-hour cycle and is popular in operations teams. Scrum cycles can be between two to four weeks and are often used by development teams using the Scrum Agile process. Longer cycles are also common and are called **Program Increments**, which span several Scrum Sprint cycles, in Scaled Agile Framework.

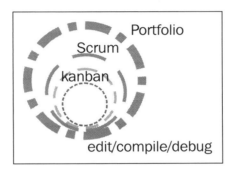

The Agile wheel of wheels

DevOps must be able to support all these cycles. This is quite natural given the central theme of DevOps: cooperation between disciplines in an Agile organization.

The most obvious and measurably concrete benefits of DevOps occur in the shorter cycles, which in turn make the longer cycles more efficient. Take care of the pennies, and the pounds will take care of themselves, as the old adage goes.

Here are some examples of when DevOps can benefit Agile cycles:

- Deployment systems, maintained by DevOps engineers, make the deliveries at the end of Scrum cycles faster and more efficient. These can take place with a periodicity of two to four weeks.

  In organizations where deployments are done mostly by hand, the time to deploy can be several days. Organizations that have these inefficient deployment processes will benefit greatly from a DevOps mindset.

- The Kanban cycle is 24 hours, and it's therefore obvious that the deployment cycle needs to be much faster than that if we are to succeed with Kanban.

  A well-designed DevOps Continuous Delivery pipeline can deploy code from being committed to the code repository to production in the order of minutes, depending on the size of the change.

Beware the cargo cult Agile fallacy

Richard Feynman was awarded the Nobel Prize for his work in the field of quantum physics in 1965. He noticed a common behavior among scientists, in which they went though all the motions of science but missed some central, vital ingredient of the scientific process. He called this behavior "cargo cult science," since it was reminiscent of the cargo cults in the Melanesian South Sea islands. These cargo cults where formed during the Second World War when the islanders watched great planes land with useful cargo. After the war stopped, the cargo also stopped coming. The islanders started simulating landing strips, doing everything just as they had observed the American military do, in order for the planes to land.

A cargo cult Agile aeroplane

We are not working in an Agile or DevOps-oriented manner simply because we have a morning stand-up where we drink coffee and chat about the weather. We don't have a DevOps pipeline just because we have a Puppet implementation that only the operations team knows anything about.

It is very important that we keep track of our goals and continuously question whether we are doing the right thing and are still on the right track. This is central to all Agile thinking. It is, however, something that is manifestly very hard to do in practice. It is easy to wind up as followers of the cargo cults.

When constructing deployment pipelines, for example, keep in mind why we are building them in the first place. The goal is to allow people to interact with new systems faster and with less work. This, in turn, helps people with different roles interact with each other more efficiently and with less turnaround.

If, on the other hand, we build a pipeline that only helps one group of people achieve their goals, for instance, the operations personnel, we have failed to achieve our basic goal.

While this is not an exact science, it pays to bear in mind that Agile cycles, such as the sprint cycle in the Scrum Agile method, normally have a method to deal with this situation. In Scrum, this is called the sprint retrospective, where the team gets together and discusses what went well and what could have gone better during the sprint. Spend some time here to make sure you are doing the right thing in your daily work.

A common problem here is that the output from the sprint retrospective isn't really acted upon. This, in turn, may be caused by the unfortunate fact that the identified problems were really caused by some other part of the organization that you don't communicate well with. Therefore, these problems come up again and again in the retrospectives and are never remedied.

If you recognize that your team is in this situation, you will benefit from the DevOps approach since it emphasizes cooperation between roles in the organization.

To summarize, try to use the mechanisms provided in the Agile methods in your methods themselves. If you are using Scrum, use the sprint retrospective mechanism to capture potential improvements. This being said, don't take the methods as gospel. Find out what works for you.

DevOps and ITIL

This section explains how DevOps and other ways of working coexist and fit together in a larger whole.

DevOps fits well together with many frameworks for Agile or Lean enterprises. Scaled Agile Framework, or SAFe® , specifically mentions DevOps. There is nearly never any disagreement between proponents of different Agile practices and DevOps since DevOps originated in the Agile environments. The story is a bit different with ITIL, though.

ITIL, which was formerly known as Information Technology Infrastructure Library, is a practice used by many large and mature organizations.

ITIL is a large framework that formalizes many aspects of the software life cycle. While DevOps and Continuous Delivery hold the view that the changesets we deliver to production should be small and happen often, at first glance, ITIL would appear to hold the opposite view. It should be noted that this isn't really true. Legacy systems are quite often monolithic, and in these cases, you need a process such as ITIL to manage the complex changes often associated with large monolithic systems.

If you are working in a large organization, the likelihood that you are working with such large monolithic legacy systems is very high.

In any case, many of the practices described in ITIL translate directly into corresponding DevOps practices. ITIL prescribes a configuration management system and a configuration management database. These types of systems are also integral to DevOps, and several of them will be described in this book.

Summary

This chapter presented a brief overview of the background of the DevOps movement. We discussed the history of DevOps and its roots in development and operations, as well as in the Agile movement. We also took a look at how ITIL and DevOps might coexist in larger organizations. The cargo cult anti-pattern was explored, and we discussed how to avoid it. You should now be able to answer where DevOps fits into a larger Agile context and the different cycles of Agile development.

We will gradually move toward more technical and hands-on subjects. The next chapter will present an overview of what the technical systems we tend to focus on in DevOps look like.

2
A View from Orbit

The DevOps process and Continuous Delivery pipelines can be very complex. You need to have a grasp of the intended final results before starting the implementation.

This chapter will help you understand how the various systems of a Continuous Delivery pipeline fit together, forming a larger whole.

In this chapter, we will read about:

- An overview of the DevOps process, a Continuous Delivery pipeline implementation, and the participants in the process
- Release management
- Scrum, Kanban, and the delivery pipeline
- Bottlenecks

The DevOps process and Continuous Delivery – an overview

There is a lot of detail in the following overview image of the Continuous Delivery pipeline, and you most likely won't be able to read all the text. Don't worry about this just now; we are going to delve deeper into the details as we go along.

For the time being, it is enough to understand that when we work with DevOps, we work with large and complex processes in a large and complex context.

An example of a Continuous Delivery pipeline in a large organization is introduced in the following image:

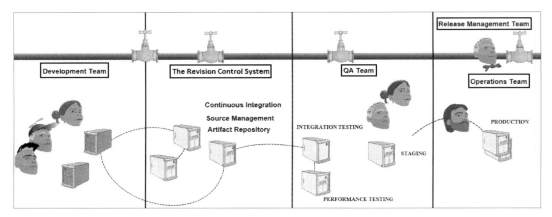

While the basic outline of this image holds true surprisingly often, regardless of the organization. There are, of course, differences, depending on the size of the organization and the complexity of the products that are being developed.

The early parts of the chain, that is, the developer environments and the Continuous Integration environment, are normally very similar.

The number and types of testing environments vary greatly. The production environments also vary greatly.

In the following sections, we will discuss the different parts of the Continuous Delivery pipeline.

The developers

The developers (on the far left in the figure) work on their workstations. They develop code and need many tools to be efficient.

The following detail from the previous larger Continuous Delivery pipeline overview illustrates the development team.

Ideally, they would each have production-like environments available to work with locally on their workstations or laptops. Depending on the type of software that is being developed, this might actually be possible, but it's more common to simulate, or rather, mock, the parts of the production environments that are hard to replicate. This might, for example, be the case for dependencies such as external payment systems or phone hardware.

When you work with DevOps, you might, depending on which of its two constituents you emphasized on in your original background, pay more or less attention to this part of the Continuous Delivery pipeline. If you have a strong developer background, you appreciate the convenience of a prepackaged developer environment, for example, and work a lot with those. This is a sound practice, since otherwise developers might spend a lot of time creating their development environments. Such a prepackaged environment might, for instance, include a specific version of the Java Development Kit and an integrated development environment, such as Eclipse. If you work with Python, you might package a specific Python version, and so on.

Keep in mind that we essentially need two or more separately maintained environments. The preceding developer environment consists of all the development tools we need. These will not be installed on the test or production systems. Further, the developers also need some way to deploy their code in a production-like way. This can be a virtual machine provisioned with Vagrant running on the developer's machine, a cloud instance running on AWS, or a Docker container: there are many ways to solve this problem.

My personal preference is to use a development environment that is similar to the production environment. If the production servers run Red Hat Linux, for instance, the development machine might run CentOS Linux or Fedora Linux. This is convenient because you can use much of the same software that you run in production locally and with less hassle. The compromise of using CentOS or Fedora can be motivated by the license costs of Red Hat and also by the fact that enterprise distributions usually lag behind a bit with software versions.

If you are running Windows servers in production, it might also be more convenient to use a Windows development machine.

The revision control system

The revision control system is often the heart of the development environment. The code that forms the organization's software products is stored here. It is also common to store the configurations that form the infrastructure here. If you are working with hardware development, the designs might also be stored in the revision control system.

The following image shows the systems dealing with code, Continuous Integration, and artifact storage in the Continuous Delivery pipeline in greater detail:

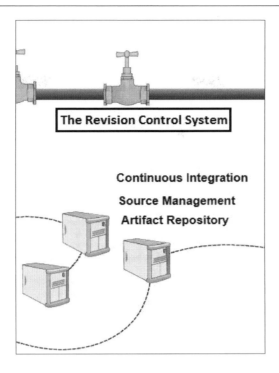

For such a vital part of the organization's infrastructure, there is surprisingly little variation in the choice of product. These days, many use Git or are switching to it, especially those using proprietary systems reaching end-of-life.

Regardless of the revision control system you use in your organization, the choice of product is only one aspect of the larger picture.

You need to decide on directory structure conventions and which branching strategy to use.

If you have a great deal of independent components, you might decide to use a separate repository for each of them.

Since the revision control system is the heart of the development chain, many of its details will be covered in *Chapter 5, Building the Code*.

The build server

The build server is conceptually simple. It might be seen as a glorified egg timer that builds your source code at regular intervals or on different triggers.

The most common usage pattern is to have the build server listen to changes in the revision control system. When a change is noticed, the build server updates its local copy of the source from the revision control system. Then, it builds the source and performs optional tests to verify the quality of the changes. This process is called Continuous Integration. It will be explored in more detail in *Chapter 5*, *Building the Code*.

Unlike the situation for code repositories, there hasn't yet emerged a clear winner in the build server field.

In this book, we will discuss Jenkins, which is a widely used open source solution for build servers. Jenkins works right out of the box, giving you a simple and robust experience. It is also fairly easy to install.

The artifact repository

When the build server has verified the quality of the code and compiled it into deliverables, it is useful to store the compiled binary artifacts in a repository. This is normally not the same as the revision control system.

In essence, these binary code repositories are filesystems that are accessible over the HTTP protocol. Normally, they provide features for searching and indexing as well as storing metadata, such as various type identifiers and version information about the artifacts.

In the Java world, a pretty common choice is Sonatype Nexus. Nexus is not limited to Java artifacts, such as Jars or Ears, but can also store artifacts of the operating system type, such as RPMs, artifacts suitable for JavaScript development, and so on.

Amazon S3 is a key-value datastore that can be used to store binary artifacts. Some build systems, such as Atlassian Bamboo, can use Amazon S3 to store artifacts. The S3 protocol is open, and there are open source implementations that can be deployed inside your own network. One such possibility is the Ceph distributed filesystem, which provides an S3-compatible object store.

Package managers, which we will look at next, are also artifact repositories at their core.

Package managers

Linux servers usually employ systems for deployment that are similar in principle but have some differences in practice.

Red Hat-like systems use a package format called RPM. Debian-like systems use the .deb format, which is a different package format with similar abilities. The deliverables can then be installed on servers with a command that fetches them from a binary repository. These commands are called package managers.

On Red Hat systems, the command is called yum, or, more recently, dnf. On Debian-like systems, it is called aptitude/dpkg.

The great benefit of these package management systems is that it is easy to install and upgrade a package; dependencies are installed automatically.

If you don't have a more advanced system in place, it would be feasible to log in to each server remotely and then type yum upgrade on each one. The newest packages would then be fetched from the binary repository and installed. Of course, as we will see, we do indeed have more advanced systems of deployment available; therefore, we won't need to perform manual upgrades.

Test environments

After the build server has stored the artifacts in the binary repository, they can be installed from there into test environments.

The following figure shows the test systems in greater detail:

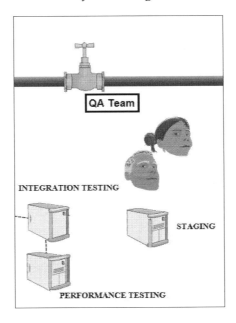

Test environments should normally attempt to be as production-like as is feasible. Therefore, it is desirable that the they be installed and configured with the same methods as production servers.

Staging/production

Staging environments are the last line of test environments. They are interchangeable with production environments. You install your new releases on the staging servers, check that everything works, and then swap out your old production servers and replace them with the staging servers, which will then become the new production servers. This is sometimes called the blue-green deployment strategy.

The exact details of how to perform this style of deployment depend on the product being deployed. Sometimes, it is not possible to have several production systems running in parallel, usually because production systems are very expensive.

At the other end of the spectrum, we might have many hundreds of production systems in a pool. We can then gradually roll out new releases in the pool. Logged-in users stay with the version running on the server they are logged in to. New users log in to servers running new versions of the software.

The following detail from the larger Continuous Delivery image shows the final systems and roles involved:

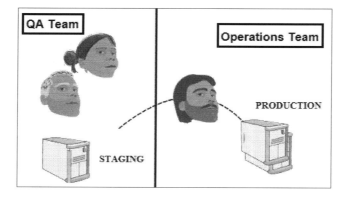

Not all organizations have the resources to maintain production-quality staging servers, but when it's possible, it is a nice and safe way to handle upgrades.

Release management

We have so far assumed that the release process is mostly automatic. This is the dream scenario for people working with DevOps.

This dream scenario is a challenge to achieve in the real world. One reason for this is that it is usually hard to reach the level of test automation needed in order to have complete confidence in automated deploys. Another reason is simply that the cadence of business development doesn't always the match cadence of technical development. Therefore, it is necessary to enable human intervention in the release process.

A faucet is used in the following figure to symbolize human interaction—in this case, by a dedicated release manager.

How this is done in practice varies, but deployment systems usually have a way to support how to describe which software versions to use in different environments.

The integration test environments can then be set to use the latest versions that have been deployed to the binary artifact repository. The staging and production servers have particular versions that have been tested by the quality assurance team.

Scrum, Kanban, and the delivery pipeline

How does the Continuous Delivery pipeline that we have described in this chapter support Agile processes such as Scrum and Kanban?

Scrum focuses on sprint cycles, which can occur biweekly or monthly. Kanban can be said to focus more on shorter cycles, which can occur daily.

The philosophical differences between Scrum and Kanban are a bit deeper, although not mutually exclusive. Many organizations use both Kanban and Scrum together.

From a software-deployment viewpoint, both Scrum and Kanban are similar. Both require frequent hassle-free deployments. From a DevOps perspective, a change starts propagating through the Continuous Delivery pipeline toward test systems and beyond when it is deemed ready enough to start that journey. This might be judged on subjective measurements or objective ones, such as "all unit tests are green."

Our pipeline can manage both the following types of scenarios:

- The build server supports the generation of the objective code quality metrics that we need in order to make decisions. These decisions can either be made automatically or be the basis for manual decisions.

- The deployment pipeline can also be directed manually. This can be handled with an issue management system, via configuration code commits, or both.

So, again, from a DevOps perspective, it doesn't really matter if we use Scrum, Scaled Agile Framework, Kanban, or another method within the lean or Agile frameworks. Even a traditional Waterfall process can be successfully managed — DevOps serves all!

Wrapping up – a complete example

So far, we have covered a lot of information at a cursory level.

To make it more clear, let's have a look at what happens to a concrete change as it propagates through the systems, using an example:

- The development team has been given the responsibility to develop a change to the organization's system. The change revolves around adding new roles to the authentication system. This seemingly simple task is hard in reality because many different systems will be affected by the change.

- To make life easier, it is decided that the change will be broken down into several smaller changes, which will be tested independently and mostly automatically by automated regression tests.

- The first change, the addition of a new role to the authentication system, is developed locally on developer machines and given best-effort local testing. To really know if it works, the developer needs access to systems not available in his or her local environment; in this case, an LDAP server containing user information and roles.

- If test-driven development is used, a failing test is written even before any actual code is written. After the failing test is written, new code that makes the test pass is written.

- The developer checks in the change to the organization's revision control system, a Git repository.

- The build server picks up the change and initiates the build process. After unit testing, the change is deemed fit enough to be deployed to the binary repository, which is a Nexus installation.

- The configuration management system, Puppet, notices that there is a new version of the authentication component available. The integration test server is described as requiring the latest version to be installed, so Puppet goes ahead and installs the new component.

- The installation of the new component now triggers automated regression tests. When these have been finished successfully, manual tests by the quality assurance team commence.

- The quality assurance team gives the change its seal of approval. The change moves on to the staging server, where final acceptance testing commences.

- After the acceptance test phase is completed, the staging server is swapped into production, and the production server becomes the new staging server. This last step is managed by the organization's load-balancing server.

The process is then repeated as needed. As you can see, there is a lot going on!

Identifying bottlenecks

As is apparent from the previous example, there is a lot going on for any change that propagates through the pipeline from development to production. It is important for this process to be efficient.

As with all Agile work, keep track of what you are doing, and try to identify problem areas.

When everything is working as it should, a commit to the code repository should result in the change being deployed to integration test servers within a 15-minute time span.

When things are not working well, a deploy can take days of unexpected hassles. Here are some possible causes:

- Database schema changes.

- Test data doesn't match expectations.

- Deploys are person dependent, and the person wasn't available.

- There is unnecessary red tape associated with propagating changes.
- Your changes aren't small and therefore require a lot of work to deploy safely. This might be because your architecture is basically a monolith.

We will examine these challenges further in the chapters ahead.

Summary

In this chapter, we delved further into the different types of systems and processes you normally work with when doing DevOps work. We gained a deeper, detailed understanding of the Continuous Delivery process, which is at the core of DevOps.

Next, we will look into how the DevOps mindset affects software architecture in order to help us achieve faster and more precise deliveries.

3
How DevOps Affects Architecture

Software architecture is a vast subject, and in this book, we will focus on the aspects of architecture that have the largest effects on Continuous Delivery and DevOps and vice versa.

In this chapter, we will see:

- Aspects of software architecture and what it means to us while working with our DevOps glasses on
- Basic terminology and goals
- Anti-patterns, such as the monolith
- The fundamental principle of the separation of concerns
- Three-tier systems and microservices

We finally conclude with some practical issues regarding database migration.

It's quite a handful, so let's get started!

Introducing software architecture

We will discuss how DevOps affects the architecture of our applications rather than the architecture of software deployment systems, which we discuss elsewhere in the book.

Often while discussing software architecture, we think of the non-functional requirements of our software. By non-functional requirements, we mean different characteristics of the software rather than the requirements on particular behaviors.

A functional requirement could be that our system should be able to deal with credit card transactions. A non-functional requirement could be that the system should be able to manage several such credit cards transactions per second.

Here are two of the non-functional requirements that DevOps and Continuous Delivery place on software architecture:

- We need to be able to deploy small changes often
- We need to be able to have great confidence in the quality of our changes

The normal case should be that we are able to deploy small changes all the way from developers' machines to production in a small amount of time. Rolling back a change because of unexpected problems caused by it should be a rare occurrence.

So, if we take out the deployment systems from the equation for a while, how will the architecture of the software systems we deploy be affected?

The monolithic scenario

One way to understand the issues that a problematic architecture can cause for Continuous Delivery is to consider a counterexample for a while.

Let's suppose we have a large web application with many different functions. We also have a static website inside the application. The entire web application is deployed as a single Java EE application archive. So, when we need to fix a spelling mistake in the static website, we need to rebuild the entire web application archive and deploy it again.

While this might be seen as a silly example, and the enlightened reader would never do such a thing, I have seen this anti-pattern live in the real world. As DevOps engineers, this could be an actual situation that we might be asked to solve.

Let's break down the consequences of this tangling of concerns. What happens when we want to correct a spelling mistake? Let's take a look:

1. We know which spelling mistake we want to correct, but in which code base do we need to do it? Since we have a monolith, we need to make a branch in our code base's revision control system. This new branch corresponds to the code that we have running in production.
2. Make the branch and correct the spelling mistake.
3. Build a new artifact with the correction. Give it a new version.
4. Deploy the new artifact to production.

Okay, this doesn't seem altogether too bad at first glance. But consider the following too:

- We made a change in the monolith that our entire business critical system comprises. If something breaks while we are deploying the new version, we lose revenue by the minute. Are we really sure that the change affects nothing else?

- It turns out that we didn't really just limit the change to correcting a spelling mistake. We also changed a number of version strings when we produced the new artifact. But changing a version string should be safe too, right? Are we sure?

The point here is that we have already spent considerable mental energy in making sure that the change is really safe. The system is so complex that it becomes difficult to think about the effects of changes, even though they might be trivial.

Now, a change is usually more complex than a simple spelling correction. Thus, we need to exercise all aspects of the deployment chain, including manual verification, for all changes to a monolith.

We are now in a place that we would rather not be.

Architecture rules of thumb

There are a number of architecture rules that might help us understand how to deal with the previous undesirable situation.

The separation of concerns

The renowned Dutch computer scientist Edsger Dijkstra first mentioned his idea of how to organize thought efficiently in his paper from 1974, *On the role of scientific thought*.

He called this idea "the separation of concerns". To this date, it is arguably the single most important rule in software design. There are many other well-known rules, but many of them follow from the idea of the separation of concerns. The fundamental principle is simply that we should consider different aspects of a system separately.

The principle of cohesion

In computer science, cohesion refers to the degree to which the elements of a software module belong together.

Cohesion can be used as a measure of how strongly related the functions in a module are.

It is desirable to have strong cohesion in a module.

We can see that strong cohesion is another aspect of the principle of the separation of concerns.

Coupling

Coupling refers to the degree of dependency between two modules. We always want low coupling between modules.

Again, we can see coupling as another aspect of the principle of the separation of concerns.

Systems with high cohesion and low coupling would automatically have separation of concerns, and vice versa.

Back to the monolithic scenario

In the previous scenario with the spelling correction, it is clear that we failed with respect to the separation of concerns. We didn't have any modularization at all, at least from a deployment point of view. The system appears to have the undesirable features of low cohesion and high coupling.

If we had a set of separate deployment modules instead, our spelling correction would most likely have affected only a single module. It would have been more apparent that deploying the change was safe.

How this should be accomplished in practice varies, of course. In this particular example, the spelling corrections probably belong to a frontend web component. At the very least, this frontend component can be deployed separately from the backend components and have their own life cycle.

In the real world though, we might not be lucky enough to always be able to influence the different technologies used by the organization where we work. The frontend might, for instance, be implemented using a proprietary content management system with quirks of its own. Where you experience such circumstances, it would be wise to keep track of the cost such a system causes.

A practical example

Let's now take a look at the concrete example we will be working on for the remainder of the book. In our example, we work for an organization called Matangle. This organization is a software as a service (SaaS) provider that sells access to educational games for schoolchildren.

As with any such provider, we will, with all likelihood, have a database containing customer information. It is this database that we will start out with.

The organization's other systems will be fleshed out as we go along, but this initial system serves well for our purposes.

Three-tier systems

The Matangle customer database is a very typical three-tier, **CRUD (create, read, update,** and **delete)** type of system. This software architecture pattern has been in use for decades and continues to be popular. These types of systems are very common, and it is quite likely that you will encounter them, either as legacy systems or as new designs.

In this figure, we can see the separation of concerns idea in action:

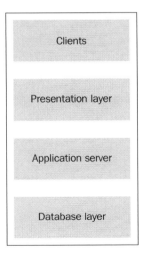

The three tiers listed as follows show examples of how our organization has chosen to build its system.

The presentation tier

The presentation tier will be a web frontend implemented using the React web framework. It will be deployed as a set of JavaScript and static HTML files. The React framework is fairly recent. Your organization might not use React but perhaps some other framework such as Angular instead. In any case, from a deployment and build point of view, most JavaScript frameworks are similar.

The logic tier

The logic tier is a backend implemented using the Clojure language on the Java platform. The Java platform is very common in large organizations, while smaller organizations might prefer other platforms based on Ruby or Python. Our example, based on Clojure, contains a little bit of both worlds.

The data tier

In our case, the database is implemented with the PostgreSQL database system. PostgreSQL is a relational database management system. While arguably not as common as MySQL installations, larger enterprises might prefer Oracle databases. PostgreSQL is, in any case, a robust system, and our example organization has chosen PostgreSQL for this reason.

From a DevOps point of view, the three-tier pattern looks compelling, at least superficially. It should be possible to deploy changes to each of the three layers separately, which would make it simple to propagate small changes through the servers.

In practice, though, the data tier and logic tier are often tightly coupled. The same might also be true for the presentation tier and logic tier. To avoid this, care must be taken to keep the interfaces between the tiers lean. Using well-known patterns isn't necessarily a panacea. If we don't take care while designing our system, we can still wind up with an undesirable monolithic system.

Handling database migrations

Handling changes in a relational database requires special consideration.

A relational database stores both data and the structure of the data. Upgrading a database schema offers other challenges then the ones present when upgrading program binaries. Usually, when we upgrade an application binary, we stop the application, upgrade it, and then start it again. We don't really bother about the application state. That is handled outside of the application.

When upgrading databases, we do need to consider state, because a database contains comparatively little logic and structure, but contains much state.

In order to describe a database structure change, we issue a command to change the structure.

The database structures before and after a change is applied should be seen as different versions of the database. How do we keep track of database versions?

Liquibase is a database migration system that, at its core, uses a tried and tested method. There are many systems like this, usually at least one for every programming language. Liquibase is well-known in the Java world, and even in the Java world, there are several alternatives that work in a similar manner. Flyway is another example for the Java platform.

Generally, database migration systems employ some variant of the following method:

- Add a table to the database where a database version is stored.
- Keep track of database change commands and bunch them together in versioned changesets. In the case of Liquibase, these changes are stored in XML files. Flyway employs a slightly different method where the changesets are handled as separate SQL files or occasionally as separate Java classes for more complex transitions.
- When Liquibase is being asked to upgrade a database, it looks at the metadata table and determines which changesets to run in order to make the database up-to-date with the latest version.

As previously stated, many database version management systems work like this. They differ mostly in the way the changesets are stored and how they determine which changesets to run. They might be stored in an XML file, like in the case of Liquibase, or as a set of separate SQL files, as with Flyway. This later method is more common with homegrown systems and has some advantages. The Clojure ecosystem also has at least one similar database migration system of its own, called Migratus.

Rolling upgrades

Another thing to consider when doing database migrations is what can be referred to as rolling upgrades. These kinds of deployments are common when you don't want your end user to experience any downtime, or at least very little downtime.

Here is an example of a rolling upgrade for our organization's customer database.

When we start, we have a running system with one database and two servers. We have a load balancer in front of the two servers.

We are going to roll out a change to the database schema, which also affects the servers. We are going to split the customer name field in the database into two separate fields, first name and surname.

This is an incompatible change. How do we minimize downtime? Let's look at the solution:

1. We start out by doing a database migration that creates the two new name fields and then fills these new fields by taking the old name field and splitting the field into two halves by finding a space character in the name. This was the initial chosen encoding for names, which wasn't stellar. This is why we want to change it.

   This change is so far backward compatible, because we didn't remove the name field; we just created two new fields that are, so far, unused.

2. Next, we change the load balancer configuration so that the second of our two servers is no longer accessible from the outside world. The first server chugs along happily, because the old name field is still accessible to the old server code.

3. Now we are free to upgrade server two, since nobody uses it.

   After the upgrade, we start it, and it is also happy because it uses the two new database fields.

4. At this point, we can again switch the load balancer configuration such that server one is not available, and server two is brought online instead. We do the same kind of upgrade on server one while it is offline. We start it and now make both servers accessible again by reinstating our original load balancer configuration.

Now, the change is deployed almost completely. The only thing remaining is removing the old name field, since no server code uses it anymore.

As we can see, rolling upgrades require a lot of work in advance to function properly. It is far easier to schedule upgrades during natural downtimes, if your organization has any. International organizations might not have any suitable natural windows to perform upgrades, and then rolling upgrades might be the only option.

Hello world in Liquibase

This is a simple "hello world" style example for the Liquibase relational database changeset handler.

To try the example out, unpack the source code bundle and run Maven, the Java build tool.

```
cd ch3-liquibase-helloworld
mvn liquibase:update
```

The changelog file

The following is an example of what a Liquibase changelog file can look like.

It defines two changesets, or migrations, with the numerical identifiers 1 and 2:

- Changeset 1 creates a table called customer, with a column called name
- Changeset 2 adds a column called address to the table called customer

```xml
<?xml version="1.0" encoding="utf-8"?>
<databaseChangeLog xmlns="http://www.liquibase.org/xml/ns/
dbchangelog"
xmlns:xsi="http://www.w3.org/2001/XMLSchema-instance"
xsi:schemaLocation="http://www.liquibase.org/xml/ns/dbchangelog
http://www.liquibase.org/xml/ns/dbchangelog/dbchangelog-3.0.xsd">

  <changeSet id="1" author="jave">

    <createTable tableName="customer">
      <column name="id" type="int"/>
      <column name="name" type="varchar(50)"/>
    </createTable>
  </changeSet>
```

```
<changeSet id="2" author="jave">
  <addColumn  tableName="customer">
     <column name="address" type="varchar(255)"/>
  </addColumn>
</changeSet>

</databaseChangeLog>
```

The pom.xml file

The pom.xml file, which is a standard Maven project model file, defines things such as the JDBC URL we need so that we can connect to the database we wish to work with as well as the version of the Liquibase plugin.

An H2 database file, /tmp/liquidhello.h2.db, will be created. H2 is a convenient in-memory database suitable for testing.

This is the pom.xml file for the "liquibase hello world" example:

```
<?xml version="1.0" encoding="utf-8"?>
<project xmlns="http://maven.apache.org/POM/4.0.0" xmlns:xsi="http://
www.w3.org/2001/XMLSchema-instance"
xsi:schemaLocation="http://maven.apache.org/POM/4.0.0 http://maven.
apache.org/xsd/maven-4.0.0.xsd">
  <modelVersion>4.0.0</modelVersion>
  <groupId>se.verona.liquibasehello</groupId>
  <artifactId>liquibasehello</artifactId>
  <version>1.0-SNAPSHOT</version>
  <build>
    <plugins>
      <plugin>
        <groupId>org.liquibase</groupId>
        <artifactId>liquibase-maven-plugin</artifactId>
        <version>3.0.0-rc1</version>
        <configuration>
          <changeLogFile>src/main/resources/db-changelog.xml
          </changeLogFile>
          <driver>org.h2.Driver</driver>
          <url>jdbc:h2:liquidhello</url>
        </configuration>
        <dependencies>
          <dependency>
            <groupId>com.h2database</groupId>
            <artifactId>h2</artifactId>
            <version>1.3.171</version>
          </dependency>
```

```
        </dependencies>
      </plugin>
    </plugins>
  </build>
</project>
```

If you run the code and everything works correctly, the result will be an H2 database file. H2 has a simple web interface, where you can verify that the database structure is indeed what you expect.

Manual installation

Before we can automate something, we need to understand the corresponding manual process.

Throughout this book, it is assumed that we are using a Red Hat based Linux distribution, such as Fedora or CentOS. Most Linux distributions are similar in principle, except that the command set used for package operations will perhaps differ a bit.

For the exercises, you can either use a physical server or a virtual machine installed in VirtualBox.

First we need the PostgreSQL relational database. Use this command:

```
dnf install postgresql
```

This will check whether there is a PostgreSQL server installed already. Otherwise, it will fetch the PostgreSQL packages from a remote yum repository and install it. So, on reflection, many of the potentially manual steps involved are already automated. We don't need to compile the software, check software versions, install dependencies, and so on. All of this is already done in advance on the Fedora project's build servers, which is very convenient.

For our own organization's software though, we will need to eventually emulate this behavior ourselves.

We will similarly also need a web server, in this case, NGINX. To install it, use the following command:

```
dnf install nginx
```

The dnf command replaces yum in Red Hat derived distributions. It is a compatible rewrite of yum that keeps the same command line interface.

The software that we are deploying, the Matangle customer relationship database, doesn't technically need a separate database and web server as such. A web server called HTTP Kit is already included within the Clojure layer of the software.

Often, a dedicated web server is used in front of servers built on Java, Python, and so on. The primary reason for this is, again, an issue with the separation of concerns; this time, it is not for the separation of logic but for non-functional requirements such as performance, load balancing, and security. A Java based web server might be perfectly capable of serving static content these days, but a native C-based web server such as Apache `httpd` or NGINX still has superior performance and more modest memory requirements. It is also common to use a frontend web server for SSL acceleration or load balancing, for instance.

Now, we have a database and a web server. At this point, we need to build and deploy our organization's application.

On your development machine, perform the following steps in the book's unpacked source archive directory:

```
cd ch3/crm1
lein build
```

We have now produced a Java archive that can be used to deploy and run the application.

Try out the application:

```
lein run
```

Point a browser to the URL presented in the console to see the web user interface.

How do we deploy the application properly on our servers? It would be nice if we could use the same commands and mechanisms as when we installed our databases and webservers. We will see how we do that in *Chapter 7, Deploying the Code*. For now, just running the application from a shell will have to suffice.

Microservices

Microservices is a recent term used to describe systems where the logic tier of the three-tier pattern is composed of several smaller services that communicate with language-agnostic protocols.

Typically, the language-agnostic protocol is HTTP based, commonly JSON REST, but this is not mandatory. There are several possibilities for the protocol layer.

This architectural design pattern lends itself well to a Continuous Delivery approach since, as we have seen, it's easier to deploy a set of smaller standalone services than a monolith.

Here is an illustration of what a microservices deployment might look like:

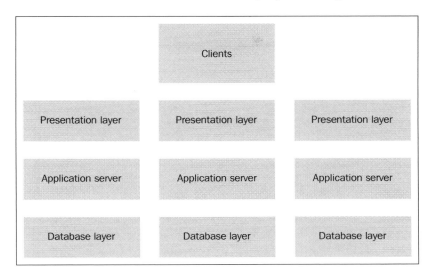

We will evolve our example towards the microservices architecture as we go along.

Interlude – Conway's Law

In 1968, Melvin Conway introduced the idea that the structure of an organization that designs software winds up copied in the organization of the software. This is called Conway's Law.

The three-tier pattern, for instance, mirrors the way many organizations' IT departments are structured:

- The database administrator team, or DBA team for short
- The backend developer team
- The frontend developer team
- The operations team

Well, that makes four teams, but we can see the resemblance clearly between the architectural pattern and the organization.

The primary goal of DevOps is to bring different roles together, preferably in cross-functional teams. If Conway's Law holds true, the organization of such teams would be mirrored in their designs.

The microservice pattern happens to mirror a cross-functional team quite closely.

How to keep service interfaces forward compatible

Service interfaces must be allowed to evolve over time. This is natural, since the organization's needs change over time, and service interfaces reflect that to a degree.

How can we accomplish this? One way is to use a pattern that is sometimes called **Tolerant Reader**. This simply means that the consumer of a service should ignore data that it doesn't recognize.

This is a method that lends itself well to REST implementations.

 SOAP, which is an XML schema-based method to define services, is more rigorous. With SOAP, you normally don't change existing interfaces. Interfaces are seen as contracts that should be constant. Instead of changing the interface, you define a new schema version. Existing consumers either have to implement the new protocol and then be deployed again, or the producer needs to provide several versioned endpoints in parallel. This is cumbersome and creates undesirable tighter coupling between providers and consumers.

While the DevOps and Continuous Delivery ideas don't actually do much in the way of mandating how things should be done, the most efficient method is usually favored.

In our example, it can be argued that the least expensive method is to spread the burden of implementing changes over both the producer and consumer. The producer needs to be changed in any case, and the consumer needs to accept a onetime cost of implementing the Tolerant Reader pattern. It is possible to do this with SOAP and XML, but it is less natural than with a REST implementation. This is one of the reasons why REST implementations are more popular in organizations where DevOps and Continuous Delivery have been embraced.

How to implement the Tolerant Reader pattern in practice varies with the platform used. For JsonRest, it's usually sufficient to parse the JSON structure into the equivalent language-specific structure. Then, you pick the parts you need for your application. All other parts, both old and new, are ignored. The limitation of this method is that the producer can't remove the parts of the structure that the consumer relies on. Adding new parts is okay, because they will be ignored.

This again puts a burden on the producer to keep track of the consumer's wishes.

Inside the walls of an organization, this isn't necessarily a big problem. The producer can keep track of copies of the consumer's latest reader code and test that they still work during the producer's build phase.

For services that are exposed to the Internet at large, this method isn't really usable, in which case the more rigorous approach of SOAP is preferable.

Microservices and the data tier

One way of viewing microservices is that each microservice is potentially a separate three-tier system. We don't normally implement each tier for each microservice though. With this in mind, we see that each microservice can implement its own data layer. The benefit would be a potential increase of separation between services.

 It is more common in my experience, though, to put all of the organization's data into a single database or at least a single database type. This is more common, but not necessarily better.

There are pros and cons to both scenarios. It is easier to deploy changes when the systems are clearly separate from each other. On the other hand, data modeling is easier when everything is stored in the same database.

DevOps, architecture, and resilience

We have seen that the microservice architecture has many desirable properties from a DevOps point of view. An important goal of DevOps is to place new features in the hands of our user faster. This is a consequence of the greater amount of modularization that microservices provide.

Those who fear that microservices could make life uninteresting by offering a perfect solution without drawbacks can take a sigh of relief, though. Microservices do offer challenges of their own.

We want to be able to deploy new code quickly, but we also want our software to be reliable.

Microservices have more integration points between systems and suffer from a higher possibility of failure than monolithic systems.

Automated testing is very important with DevOps so that the changes we deploy are of good quality and can be relied upon. This is, however, not a solution to the problem of services that suddenly stop working for other reasons. Since we have more running services with the microservice pattern, it is statistically more likely for a service to fail.

We can partially mitigate this problem by making an effort to monitor the services and take appropriate action when something fails. This should preferably be automated.

In our customer database example, we can employ the following strategy:

- We use two application servers that both run our application
- The application offers a special monitoring interface via JsonRest
- A monitoring daemon periodically polls this monitoring interface
- If a server stops working, the load balancer is reconfigured such that the offending server is taken out of the server pool

This is obviously a simple example, but it serves to illustrate the challenges we face when designing resilient systems that comprise many moving parts and how they might affect architectural decisions.

Why do we offer our own application-specific monitoring interface though? Since the purpose of monitoring is to give us a thorough understanding of the current health of the system, we normally monitor many aspects of the application stack. We monitor that the server CPU isn't overloaded, that there is sufficient disk and memory space available, and that the base application server is running. This might not be sufficient to determine whether a service is running properly, though. For instance, the service might for some reason have a broken database access configuration. A service-specific health probing interface would attempt to contact the database and return the status of the connection in the return structure.

It is, of course, best if your organization can agree on a common format for the probing return structure. The structure will also depend on the type of monitoring software used.

Summary

In this chapter, we took a look at the vast subject of software architecture from the viewpoint of DevOps and Continuous Delivery.

We learned about the many different faces that the rule of the separation of concerns can take. We also started working on the deployment strategy for one component within our organization, the Matangle customer database.

We delved into details, such as how to install software from repositories and how to manage database changes. We also had a look at high level subjects such as classic three-tier systems and the more recent microservices concept.

Our next stop will deal with how to manage source code and set up a source code revision control system.

4
Everything is Code

Everything is code, and you need somewhere to store it. The organization's source code management system is that place.

Developers and operations personnel share the same central storage for their different types of code.

There are many ways of hosting the central code repository:

- You can use a software as a service solution, such as GitHub, Bitbucket, or GitLab. This can be cost-effective and provide good availability.
- You can use a cloud provider, such as AWS or Rackspace, to host your repositories.

Some types of organization simply can't let their code leave the building. For them, a private in-house setup is the best choice.

In this chapter, we will explore different options, such as Git, and web-based frontends to Git, such as Gerrit and GitLab.

This exploration will serve to help you find a Git hosting solution that covers your organization's needs.

In this chapter, we will start to experience one of the challenges in the field of DevOps—there are so many solutions to choose from and explore! This is particularly true for the world of source code management, which is central to the DevOps world.

Therefore, we will also introduce the software virtualization tool Docker from a user's perspective so that we can use the tool in our exploration.

The need for source code control

Terence McKenna, an American author, once said that everything is code.

While one might not agree with McKenna about whether everything in the universe can be represented as code, for DevOps purposes, indeed nearly everything can be expressed in codified form, including the following:

- The applications that we build
- The infrastructure that hosts our applications
- The documentation that documents our products

Even the hardware that runs our applications can be expressed in the form of software.

Given the importance of code, it is only natural that the location that we place code, the source code repository, is central to our organization. Nearly everything we produce travels through the code repository at some point in its life cycle.

The history of source code management

In order to understand the central need for source code control, it can be illuminating to have a brief look at the development history of source code management. This gives us an insight into the features that we ourselves might need. Some examples are as follows:

- Storing historical versions of source in separate archives.

  This is the simplest form, and it still lives on to some degree, with many free software projects offering tar archives of older releases to download.

- Centralized source code management with check in and check out.

  In some systems, a developer can lock files for exclusive use. Every file is managed separately. Tools like this include RCS and SCCS.

> Normally, you don't encounter this class of tool anymore, except the occasional file header indicating that a file was once managed by RCS.

- A centralized store where you merge before you commit. Examples include **Concurrent Versions System (CVS)** and **Subversion**.

Subversion in particular is still in heavy use. Many organizations have centralized workflows, and Subversion implements such workflows well enough for them.

* A decentralized store.

    On each step of the evolutionary ladder, we are offered more flexibility and concurrency as well as faster and more efficient workflows. We are also offered more advanced and powerful guns to shoot ourselves in the foot with, which we need to keep in mind!

Currently, Git is the most popular tool in this class, but there are many other similar tools in use, such as Bazaar and Mercurial.

Time will tell whether Git and its underlying data model will fend off the contenders to the throne of source code management, who will undoubtedly manifest themselves in the coming years.

Roles and code

From a DevOps point of view, it is important to leverage the natural meeting point that a source code management tool is. Many different roles have a use for source code management in its wider meaning. It is easier to do so for technically-minded roles but harder for other roles, such as project management.

Developers live and breathe source code management. It's their bread and butter.

Operations personnel also favor managing the descriptions of infrastructure in the form of code, scripts, and other artifacts, as we will see in the coming chapters. Such infrastructural descriptors include network topology, versions of software that should be installed on particular servers, and so on.

Quality assurance personnel can store their automated tests in codified form in the source code repository. This is true for software testing frameworks such as Selenium and Junit, among others.

There is a problem with the documentation of the manual steps needed to perform various tasks, though. This is more of a psychological or cultural problem than a technical one.

While many organizations employ a wiki solution such as the wiki engine powering Wikipedia, there is still a lot of documentation floating around in the Word format on shared drives and in e-mails.

This makes documentation hard to find and use for some roles and easy for others. From a DevOps viewpoint, this is regrettable, and an effort should be made so that all roles can have good and useful access to the documentation in the organization.

It is possible to store all documentation in the wiki format in the central source code repository, depending on the wiki engine used.

Which source code management system?

There are many source code management (SCM) systems out there, and since SCM is such an important part of development, the development of these systems will continue to happen.

Currently, there is a dominant system, however, and that system is Git.

Git has an interesting story: it was initiated by Linus Torvalds to move Linux kernel development from BitKeeper, which was a proprietary system used at the time. The license of BitKeeper changed, so it wasn't practical to use it for the kernel anymore.

Git therefore supports the fairly complicated workflow of Linux kernel development and is, at the base technical level, good enough for most organizations.

The primary benefit of Git versus older systems is that it is a distributed version control system (DVCS). There are many other distributed version control systems, but Git is the most pervasive one.

Distributed version control systems have several advantages, including, but not limited to, the following:

- It is possible to use a DVCS efficiently even when not connected to a network. You can take your work with you when traveling on a train or an intercontinental flight.

- Since you don't need to connect to a server for every operation, a DVCS can be faster than the alternatives in most scenarios.

- You can work privately until you feel your work is ready enough to be shared.

- It is possible to work with several remote logins simultaneously, which avoids a single point of failure.

Other distributed version control systems apart from Git include the following:

- **Bazaar**: This is abbreviated as bzr. Bazaar is endorsed and supported by Canonical, which is the company behind Ubuntu. Launchpad, which is Canonical's code hosting service, supports Bazaar.
- **Mercurial**: Notable open source projects such as Firefox and OpenJDK use Mercurial. It originated around the same time as Git.

Git can be complex, but it makes up for this by being fast and efficient. It can be hard to understand, but that can be made easier by using frontends that support different tasks.

A word about source code management system migrations

I have worked with many source code management systems and experienced many transitions from one type of system to another.

Sometimes, much time is spent on keeping all the history intact while performing a migration. For some systems, this effort is well spent, such as for venerable free or open source projects.

For many organizations, keeping the history is not worth the significant expenditure in time and effort. If an older version is needed at some point, the old source code management system can be kept online and referenced. This includes migrations from Visual SourceSafe and ClearCase.

Some migrations are trivial though, such as moving from Subversion to Git. In these cases, historic accuracy need not be sacrificed.

Choosing a branching strategy

When working with code that deploys to servers, it is important to agree on a branching strategy across the organization.

A branching strategy is a convention, or a set of rules, that describes when branches are created, how they are to be named, what use branches should have, and so on.

Branching strategies are important when working together with other people and are, to a degree, less important when you are working on your own, but they still have a purpose.

Most source code management systems do not prescribe a particular branching strategy and neither does Git. The SCM simply gives you the base mechanics to perform branching.

With Git and other distributed version control systems, it is usually pretty cheap to work locally with feature branches. A feature, or topic, branch is a branch that is used to keep track of ongoing development regarding a particular feature, bug, and so on. This way, all changes in the code regarding the feature can be handled together.

There are many well-known branching strategies. Vincent Driessen formalized a branching strategy called **Git flow**, which has many good features. For some, Git flow is too complex, and in those cases, it can be scaled down. There are many such scaled-down models available. This is what Git flow looks like:

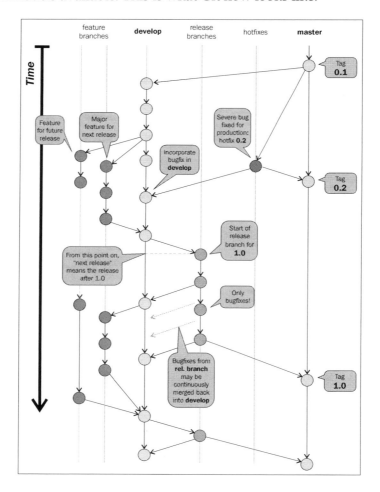

Git flow looks complex, so let's have a brief look at what the branches are for:

- The **master** branch only contains finished work. All commits are tagged, since they represent releases. All releases happen from **master**.

- The **develop** branch is where work on the next release happens. When work is finished here, **develop** is merged to master.

- We use separate **feature branches** for all new features. **Feature branches** are merged to develop.

- When a devastating bug is revealed in production, a **hotfix** branch is made where a bug fix is created. The **hotfix** branch is then merged to **master**, and a new release for production is made.

Git flow is a centralized pattern, and as such, it's reminiscent of the workflows used with Subversion, CVS, and so on. The main difference is that using Git has some technical and efficiency-related advantages.

Another strategy, called the forking pattern, where every developer has a central repository, is rarely used in practice within organizations, except when, for instance, external parties such as subcontractors are being employed.

Branching problem areas

There is a source of contention between Continuous Delivery practices and branching strategies. Some Continuous Delivery methods advocate a single master branch and all releases being made from the master branch. Git flow is one such model.

This simplifies some aspects of deployment, primarily because the branching graph becomes simpler. This in turn leads to simplified testing, because there is only one branch that leads to the production servers.

On the other hand, what if we need to perform a bug fix on released code, and the master has new features we don't want to release yet? This happens when the installation cadence in production is slower than the release cadence of the development teams. It is an undesirable state of affairs, but not uncommon.

There are two basic methods of handling this issue:

- **Make a bug fix branch and deploy to production from it**: This is simpler in the sense that we don't disrupt the development flow. On the other hand, this method might require duplication of testing resources. They might need to mirror the branching strategy.

- **Feature toggling**: Another method that places harder requirements on the developers is feature toggling. In this workflow, you turn off features that are not yet ready for production. This way you can release the latest development version, including the bug fix, together with new features, which will be disabled and inactive.

There are no hard rules, and dogmatism is not helpful in this case.

It is better to prepare for both scenarios and use the method that serves you best in the given circumstances.

Here are some observations to guide you in your choice:

Feature toggling is good when you have changes that are mostly backward compatible or are entirely new. Otherwise, the feature toggling code might become overly complex, catering to many different cases. This, in turn, complicates testing.

Bug fix branches complicate deployment and testing. While it is straightforward to branch and make the bug fix, what should the new version be called, and where do we test it? The testing resources are likely to already be occupied by ongoing development branches.

Some products are simple enough for us to create testing environments on the fly as needed, but this is rarely the case with more complex applications. Sometimes, testing resources are very scarce, such as third party web services that are difficult to copy or even hardware resources.

Artifact version naming

Version numbers become important when you have larger installations.

The following list shows the basic principles of version naming:

- Version numbers should grow monotonically, that is, become larger
- They should be comparable to each other, and it should be easy to see which version is newer
- Use the same scheme for all your artifacts

This usually translates to a version number with three or four parts:

- The first is major—changes here signal major changes in the code
- The second is for minor changes, which are backward API compatible
- The third is for bug fixes
- The fourth can be a build number

While this might seem simple, it is a sufficiently complex area to have created a standardization effort in the form of SemVer, or Semantic Versioning. The full specification can be read at `http://semver.org`.

It is convenient that all installable artifacts have a proper release number and a corresponding tag in the source code management system.

Some tools don't work this way. Maven, the Java build tool, supports a snapshot release number. A snapshot can be seen as a version with a fuzzy last part. Snapshots have a couple of drawbacks, though; for instance, you can't immediately see which source code tag the artifact corresponds to. This makes debugging broken installations harder.

The snapshot artifact strategy further violates a basic testing tenet: the exact same binary artifact that was tested should be the one that is deployed to production.

When you are working with snapshots, you instead test the snapshot until you are done testing, then you release the artifact with a real version number, and that artifact is then deployed. It is no longer the same artifact.

 While the basic idea of snapshots is, of course, that changing a version number has no practical consequences, Murphy's law states that there are, of course, consequences. It is my experience that Murphy is correct in this case, and snapshot versioning creates more harm than good. Instead, use build numbers.

Choosing a client

One of the nice aspects of Git is that it doesn't mandate the use of a particular client. There are several to choose from, and they are all compatible with each other. Most of the clients use one of several core Git implementations, which is good for stability and quality.

Most current development environments have good support for using Git.

In this sense, choosing a client is not something we actually need to do. Most clients work well enough, and the choice can be left to the preferences of those using the client. Many developers use the client integrated in their development environments, or the command-line Git client. When working with operations tasks, the command-line Git client is often preferred because it is convenient to use when working remotely through an SSH shell.

The one exception where we actually have to make a choice is when we assist people in the organization who are new to source code management in general and Git in particular.

In these cases, it is useful to maintain instructions on how to install and use a simple Git client and configure it for our organization's servers.

A simple instruction manual in the organization's wiki normally solves this issue nicely.

Setting up a basic Git server

It's pretty easy to set up a basic Git server. While this is rarely enough in a large organization, it is a good exercise before moving on to more advanced solutions.

Let's first of all specify an overview of the steps we will take and the bits and pieces we will need to complete them:

1. A client machine with two user accounts. The git and ssh packages should be installed.

    The SSH protocol features prominently as a base transport for other protocols, which is also is the case for Git.

    You need your SSH public keys handy. If you don't have the keys for some reason, use ssh-keygen to create them.

     We need two users, because we will simulate two users talking to a central server. Make keys for both test users.

2. A server where the SSH daemon is running.

    This can be the same machine as the one where you simulate the two different client users, or it can be another machine.

3. A Git server user.

   We need a separate Git user who will handle the Git server functionality.

   Now, you need to append the public keys for your two users to the `authorized_keys` file, which is located in the respective user's `.ssh` directory. Copy the keys to this account .

 Are you starting to get the feeling that all of this is a lot of hassle? This is why we will have a look at solutions that simplify this process later.

4. A bare Git repository.

   Bare Git repositories are a Git peculiarity. They are just Git repositories, except there is no working copy, so they save a bit of space. Here's how to create one:

```
cd /opt/git
mkdir project.git
cd project.git
git init --bare
```

5. Now, try cloning, making changes, and pushing to the server.

   Let's review the solution:

   ○ This solution doesn't really scale very well.

      If you have just a couple of people requiring access, the overhead of creating new projects and adding new keys isn't too bad. It's just a onetime cost. If you have a lot of people in your organization who need access, this solution requires too much work.

   ○ Solving security issues involve even more hassle.

      While I am of the perhaps somewhat controversial opinion that too much work is spent within organizations limiting employee access to systems, there is no denying that you need this ability in your setup.

      In this solution, you would need to set up separate Git server accounts for each role, and that would be a lot of duplication of effort. Git doesn't have fine-grained user access control out of the box.

Shared authentication

In most organizations, there is some form of a central server for handling authentication. An LDAP server is a fairly common choice. While it is assumed that your organization has already dealt with this core issue one way or the other and is already running an LDAP server of some sort, it is comparatively easy to set up an LDAP server for testing purposes.

One possibility is using 389 Server, named after the port commonly used for the LDAP server, together with the phpLDAPadmin web application for administration of the LDAP server.

Having this test LDAP server setup is useful for the purposes of this book, since we can then use the same LDAP server for all the different servers we are going to investigate.

Hosted Git servers

Many organizations can't use services hosted within another organization's walls at all.

These might be government organizations or organizations dealing with money, such as bank, insurance, and gaming organizations.

The causes might be legal or, simply nervousness about letting critical code leave the organization's doors, so to speak.

If you have no such qualms, it is quite reasonable to use a hosted service, such as GitHub or GitLab, that offers private accounts.

Using GitHub or GitLab is, at any rate, a convenient way to get to learn to use Git and explore its possibilities.

Both vendors are easy to evaluate, given that they offer free accounts where you can get to know the services and what they offer. See if you really need all the services or if you can make do with something simpler.

Some of the features offered by both GitLab and GitHub over plain Git are as follows:

- Web interfaces
- A documentation facility with an inbuilt wiki
- Issue trackers
- Commit visualization

- Branch visualization
- The pull request workflow

While these are all useful features, it's not always the case that you can use the facilities provided. For instance, you might already have a wiki, a documentation system, an issue tracker, and so on that you need to integrate with.

The most important features we are looking for, then, are those most closely related to managing and visualizing code.

Large binary files

GitHub and GitLab are pretty similar but do have some differences. One of them springs from the fact that source code systems like Git traditionally didn't cater much for the storage of large binary files. There have always been other ways, such as storing file paths to a file server in plain text files.

But what if you actually have files that are, in a sense, equivalent to source files except that they are binary, and you still want to version them? Such file types might include image files, video files, audio files, and so on. Modern websites make increasing use of media files, and this area has typically been the domain of content management systems (CMSes). CMSes, however nice they might be, have disadvantages compared to DevOps flows, so the allure of storing media files in your ordinary source handling system is strong. Disadvantages of CMSes include the fact that they often have quirky or nonexistent scripting capabilities. Automation, another word that should have really been included in the "DevOps" portmanteau, is therefore often difficult with a CMS.

You can, of course, just check in your binary to Git, and it will be handled like any other file. What happens then is that Git operations involving server operations suddenly become sluggish. And then, some of the main advantages of Git—efficiency and speed—vanish out the window.

Solutions to this problem have evolved over time, but there are no clear winners yet. The contenders are as follows:

- **Git LFS**, supported by GitHub
- **Git Annex**, supported by GitLab but only in the enterprise edition

Git Annex is the more mature of these. Both solutions are open source and are implemented as extensions to Git via its plugin mechanism.

There are several other systems, which indicates that this is an unresolved pain point in the current state of Git. The Git Annex has a comparison between the different breeds at `http://git-annex.branchable.com/not/`.

If you need to perform version control of your media files, you should start by exploring Git Annex. It is written in Haskell and is available through the package system of many distributions.

It should also be noted that the primary benefit of this type of solution is the ability to version media files together with the corresponding code. When working with code, you can examine the differences between versions of code conveniently. Examining differences between media files is harder and less useful.

In a nutshell, Git Annex uses a tried and tested solution to data logical problems: adding a layer of indirection. It does this by storing symlinks to files in the repository. The binary files are then stored in the filesystem and fetched by local workspaces using other means, such as rsync. This involves more work to set up the solution, of course.

Trying out different Git server implementations

The distributed nature of Git makes it possible to try out different Git implementations for various purposes. The client-side setup will be similar regardless of how the server is set up.

You can also have several solutions running in parallel. The client side is not unduly complicated by this, since Git is designed to handle several remotes if need be.

Docker intermission

In *Chapter 7, Deploying the Code*, we will have a look at a new and exciting way to package our applications, called **Docker**.

In this chapter, we have a similar challenge to solve. We need to be able to try out a couple of different Git server implementations to see which one suits our organization best.

We can use Docker for this, so we will take this opportunity to peek at the possibilities of simplified deployments that Docker offers us.

Since we are going to delve deeper into Docker further along, we will cheat a bit in this chapter and claim that Docker is used to download and run software. While this description isn't entirely untrue, Docker is much more than that. To get started with Docker, follow these steps:

1. To begin with, install Docker according to the particular instructions for your operating system. For Red Hat derivatives, it's a simple `dnf install docker-io` command.

 The `io` suffix might seem a bit mysterious, but there was already a Docker package that implemented desktop functionality, so `docker-io` was chosen instead.

2. Then, the `docker` service needs to be running:

```
systemctl enable docker
systemctl start docker
```

3. We need another tool, Docker Compose, which, at the time of writing, isn't packaged for Fedora. If you don't have it available in your package repositories, follow the instructions on this page `https://docs.docker.com/compose/install/`

 Docker Compose is used to automatically start several Docker-packaged applications, such as a database server and a web server, together, which we need for the GitLab example.

Gerrit

A basic Git server is good enough for many purposes.

Sometimes, you need precise control over the workflow, though.

One concrete example is merging changes into configuration code for critical parts of the infrastructure. While my opinion is that it's core to DevOps to not place unnecessary red tape around infrastructure code, there is no denying that it's sometimes necessary. If nothing else, developers might feel nervous committing changes to the infrastructure and would like for someone more experienced to review the code changes.

Gerrit is a Git-based code review tool that can offer a solution in these situations. In brief, Gerrit allows you to set up rules to allow developers to review and approve changes made to a codebase by other developers. These might be senior developers reviewing changes made by inexperienced developers or the more common case, which is simply that more eyeballs on the code is good for quality in general.

Gerrit is Java-based and uses a Java-based Git implementation under the hood.

Gerrit can be downloaded as a Java WAR file and has an integrated setup method. It needs a relational database as a dependency, but you can opt to use an integrated Java-based H2 database that is good enough for evaluating Gerrit.

An even simpler method is using Docker to try out Gerrit. There are several Gerrit images on the Docker registry hub to choose from. The following one was selected for this evaluation exercise: `https://hub.docker.com/r/openfrontier/gerrit/`

To run a Gerrit instance with Docker, follow these steps:

1. Initialize and start Gerrit:

   ```
   docker run -d -p 8080:8080 -p 29418:29418 openfrontier/gerrit
   ```

2. Open your browser to `http://<docker host url>:8080`

   Now, we can try out the code review feature we would like to have.

Installing the git-review package

Install `git-review` on your local installation:

```
sudo dnf install git-review
```

This will install a helper application for Git to communicate with Gerrit. It adds a new command, `git-review`, that is used instead of `git push` to push changes to the Gerrit Git server.

The value of history revisionism

When we work with code together with other people in a team, the code's history becomes more important than when we work on our own. The history of changes to files becomes a way to communicate. This is especially important when working with code review and code review tools such as Gerrit .

The code changes also need to be easy to understand. Therefore, it is useful, although perhaps counterintuitive, to edit the history of the changes in order to make the resulting history clearer.

As an example, consider a case where you made a number of changes and later changed your mind and removed them. It is not useful information for someone else that you made a set of edits and then removed them. Another case is when you have a set of commits that are easier to understand if they are a single commit. Adding commits together in this way is called **squashing** in the Git documentation.

Another case that complicates history is when you merge from the upstream central repository several times, and merge commits are added to the history. In this case, we want to simplify the changes by first removing our local changes, then fetching and applying changes from the upstream repository, and then finally reapplying our local changes. This process is called **rebasing**.

Both squashing and rebasing apply to Gerrit.

The changes should be clean, preferably one commit. This isn't something that is particular to Gerrit; it's easier for a reviewer to understand your changes if they are packaged nicely. The review will be based on this commit.

1. To begin with, we need to have the latest changes from the Git/Gerrit server side. We rebase our changes on top of the server-side changes:

    ```
    git pull --rebase origin master
    ```

2. Then, we polish our local commits by squashing them:

    ```
    git rebase -i origin/master
    ```

Now, let's have a look at the Gerrit web interface:

We can now approve the change, and it is merged to the master branch.

There is much to explore in Gerrit, but these are the basic principles and should be enough to base an evaluation on.

Are the results worth the hassle, though? These are my observations:

- Gerrit allows fine-grained access to sensitive codebases. Changes can go in after being reviewed by authorized personnel.

  This is the primary benefit of Gerrit. If you just want to have mandatory code reviews for unclear reasons, don't. The benefit has to be clear for everyone involved. It's better to agree on other more informal methods of code review than an authoritative system.

- If the alternative to Gerrit is to not allow access to code bases at all, even read-only access, then implement Gerrit.

Some parts of an organization might be too nervous to allow access to things such as infrastructure configuration. This is usually for the wrong reasons. The problem you usually face isn't people taking an interest in your code; it's the opposite.

Sometimes, sensitive passwords are checked in to code, and this is taken as a reason to disallow access to the source. Well, if it hurts, don't do it. Solve the problem that leads to there being passwords in the repositories instead.

The pull request model

There is another solution to the problem of creating workflows around code reviews: the pull request model, which has been made popular by GitHub.

In this model, pushing to repositories can be disallowed except for the repository owners. Other developers are allowed to fork the repository, though, and make changes in their fork. When they are done making changes, they can submit a pull request. The repository owners can then review the request and opt to pull the changes into the master repository.

This model has the advantage of being easy to understand, and many developers have experience in it from the many open source projects on GitHub.

Setting up a system capable of handling a pull request model locally will require something like GitHub or GitLab, which we will look at next.

GitLab

GitLab supports many convenient features on top of Git. It's a large and complex software system based on Ruby. As such, it can be difficult to install, what with getting all the dependencies right and so on.

There is a nice Docker Compose file for GitLab available at `https://registry.hub.docker.com/u/sameersbn/gitlab/`. If you followed the instructions for Docker shown previously, including the installation of `docker-compose`, it's now pretty simple to start a local GitLab instance:

```
mkdir gitlab
cd gitlab
wget https://raw.githubusercontent.com/sameersbn/docker-gitlab/master/
docker-compose.yml
docker-compose up
```

The `docker-compose` command will read the `.yml` file and start all the required services in a default demonstration configuration.

If you read the startup log in the console window, you will notice that three separate application containers have been started: `gitlab postgresql1`, `gitlab redis1`, and `gitlab gitlab1`.

The GitLab container includes the Ruby base web application and Git backend functionality. Redis is distributed key-value store, and PostgreSQL is a relational database.

If you are used to setting up complicated server functionality, you will appreciate that we have saved a great deal of time with `docker-compose`.

The `docker-compose.yml` file sets up data volumes at `/srv/docker/gitlab`.

To log in to the web user interface, use the administrator password given with the installation instructions for the GitLab Docker image. They have been replicated here, but beware that they might change as the Docker image author sees fit:

- Username: root
- Password: 5iveL!fe

Here is a screenshot of the GitLab web user interface login screen:

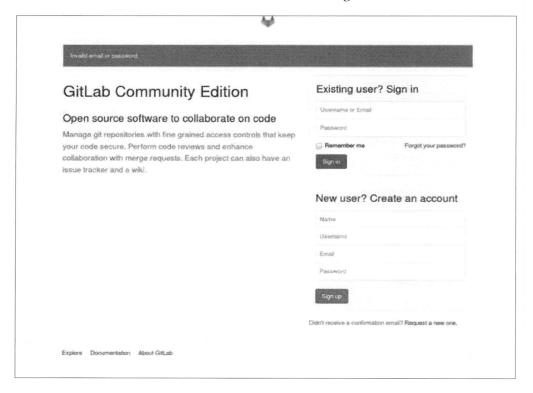

Try importing a project to your GitLab server from, for instance, GitHub or a local private project.

Have a look at how GitLab visualizes the commit history and branches.

While investigating GitLab, you will perhaps come to agree that it offers a great deal of interesting functionality.

When evaluating features, it's important to keep in mind whether it's likely that they will be used after all. What core problem would GitLab, or similar software, solve for you?

It turns out that the primary value added by GitLab, as exemplified by the following two features, is the elimination of bottlenecks in DevOps workflows:

- The management of user ssh keys
- The creation of new repositories

These features are usually deemed to be the most useful.

Visualization features are also useful, but the client-side visualization available with Git clients is more useful to developers.

Summary

In this chapter, we explored some of the options available to us for managing our organization's source code. We also investigated areas where decisions need to be made within DevOps, version numbering, and branching strategies.

After having dealt with source code in its pure form, we will next work on building the code into useful binary artifacts.

5
Building the Code

You need a system to build your code, and you need somewhere to build it.

Jenkins is a flexible open source build server that grows with your needs. Some alternatives to Jenkins will be explored as well.

We will also explore the different build systems and how they affect our DevOps work.

Why do we build code?

Most developers are familiar with the process of building code. When we work in the field of DevOps, however, we might face issues that developers who specialize in programming a particular component type won't necessarily experience.

For the purposes of this book, we define software building as the process of molding code from one form to another. During this process, several things might happen:

- The compilation of source code to native code or virtual machine bytecode, depending on our production platform.

- Linting of the code: checking the code for errors and generating code quality measures by means of static code analysis. The term "Linting" originated with a program called Lint, which started shipping with early versions of the Unix operating system. The purpose of the program was to find bugs in programs that were syntactically correct, but contained suspicious code patterns that could be identified with a different process than compiling.

- Unit testing, by running the code in a controlled manner.

- The generation of artifacts suitable for deployment.

It's a tall order!

Not all code goes through each and every one of these phases. Interpreted languages, for example, might not need compilation, but they might benefit from quality checks.

The many faces of build systems

There are many build systems that have evolved over the history of software development. Sometimes, it might feel as if there are more build systems than there are programming languages.

Here is a brief list, just to get a feeling for how many there are:

- For Java, there is Maven, Gradle, and Ant
- For C and C++, there is Make in many different flavors
- For Clojure, a language on the JVM, there is Leiningen and Boot apart from Maven
- For JavaScript, there is Grunt
- For Scala, there is sbt
- For Ruby, we have Rake
- Finally, of course, we have shell scripts of all kinds

Depending on the size of your organization and the type of product you are building, you might encounter any number of these tools. To make life even more interesting, it's not uncommon for organizations to invent their own build tools.

As a reaction to the complexity of the many build tools, there is also often the idea of standardizing a particular tool. If you are building complex heterogeneous systems, this is rarely efficient. For example, building JavaScript software is just easier with Grunt than it is with Maven or Make, building C code is not very efficient with Maven, and so on. Often, the tool exists for a reason.

Normally, organizations standardize on a single ecosystem, such as Java and Maven or Ruby and Rake. Other build systems besides those that are used for the primary code base are encountered mainly for native components and third-party components.

At any rate, we cannot assume that we will encounter only one build system within our organization's code base, nor can we assume only one programming language.

I have found this rule useful in practice: *it should be possible for a developer to check out the code and build it with minimal surprises on his or her local developer machine.*

This implies that we should standardize the revision control system and have a single interface to start builds locally.

If you have more than one build system to support, this basically means that you need to wrap one build system in another. The complexities of the build are thus hidden and more than one build system at the same time are allowed. Developers not familiar with a particular build can still expect to check it out and build it with reasonable ease.

Maven, for example, is good for declarative Java builds. Maven is also capable of starting other builds from within Maven builds.

This way, the developer in a Java-centric organization can expect the following command line to always build one of the organization's components:

```
mvn clean install
```

One concrete example is creating a Java desktop application installer with the Nullsoft NSIS Windows installation system. The Java components are built with Maven. When the Java artifacts are ready, Maven calls the NSIS installer script to produce a self-contained executable that will install the application on Windows.

While Java desktop applications are not fashionable these days, they continue to be popular in some domains.

The Jenkins build server

A build server is, in essence, a system that builds software based on various triggers. There are several to choose from. In this book, we will have a look at Jenkins, which is a popular build server written in Java.

Jenkins is a fork of the Hudson build server. Kohsuke Kawaguchi was Hudson's principal contributor, and in 2010, after Oracle acquired Hudson, he continued work on the Jenkins fork. Jenkins is clearly the more successful of the two strains today.

Jenkins has special support for building Java code but is in no way limited to just building Java.

Setting up a basic Jenkins server is not particularly hard at the outset. In Fedora, you can just install it via `dnf`:

```
dnf install jenkins
```

Jenkins is handled as a service via `systemd`:

```
systemctl start jenkins
```

You can now have a look at the web interface at `http://localhost:8080:`

The Jenkins instance in the screenshot has a couple of jobs already defined. The fundamental entity in Jenkins is the job definition, and there are several types to choose from. Let's create a simple job in the web interface. To keep it simple, this job will just print a classic Unix `fortune` quote:

1. Create a job of the type **Freestyle project**:

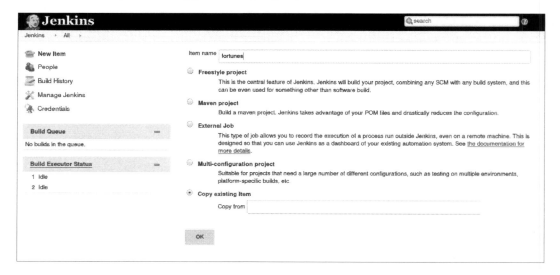

2. Add a **shell build** step.

3. In the shell entry (Command), type `fortune`:

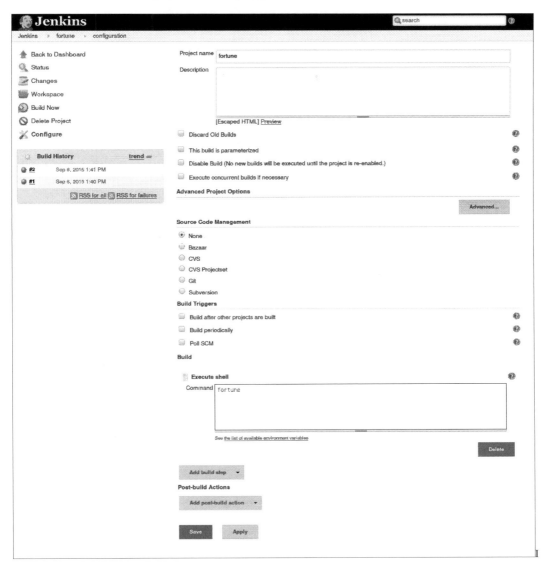

Whenever you run the job, a `fortune` quote will be printed in the job log.

Jobs can be started manually, and you will find a history of job executions and can examine each job log. This keeps a history of previous executions, which is very handy when you are trying to figure out which change broke a build and how to fix it.

If you don't have the `fortune` command, install it with `dnf install fortune-mod`, or you might opt to simply run the `date` command instead. This will just output the date in the build log instead of classic quotes and witticisms.

Managing build dependencies

In the previous, simple example, we printed a fortune cookie to the build log.

While this exercise can't be compared in complexity with managing real builds, we at least learned to install and start Jenkins, and if you had issues installing the `fortune` utility, you got a glimpse of the dark underbelly of managing a Continuous Integration server: managing the build dependencies.

Some build systems, such as the Maven tool, are nice in the way that the Maven POM file contains descriptions of which build dependencies are needed, and they are fetched automatically by Maven if they aren't already present on the build server. Grunt works in a similar way for JavaScript builds. There is a build description file that contains the dependencies required for the build. Golang builds can even contain links to GitHub repositories required for completing the build.

C and C++ builds present challenges in a different way. Many projects use GNU Autotools; among them is Autoconf, which adapts itself to the dependencies that are available on the host rather than describing which dependencies they need. So, to build Emacs, a text editor, you first run a configuration script that determines which of the many potential dependencies are available on the build system.

 If an optional dependency is missing, such as image libraries for image support, the optional feature will not be available in the final executable. You can still build the program, but you won't get features that your build machine isn't prepared for.

While this is a useful feature if you want your software to work in many different configurations depending on which system it should run on, it's not often the way we would like our builds to behave in an enterprise setting. In this case, we need to be perfectly sure which features will be available in the end. We certainly don't want bad surprises in the form of missing functionality on our production servers.

The RPM (short for Red Hat Package Manager) system, which is used on systems derived from Red Hat, offers a solution to this problem. At the core of the RPM system is a build descriptor file called a spec file, short for specification file. It lists, among other things, the build dependencies required for a successful build and the build commands and configuration options used. Since a spec file is essentially a macro-based shell script, you can use it to build many types of software. The RPM system also has the idea that build sources should be pristine. The spec file can adapt the source code by patching the source before building it.

The final artifact

After finishing the build using the RPM system, you get an RPM file, which is a very convenient type of deployment artifact for operating systems based on Red Hat. For Debian-based distributions, you get a `.deb` file.

The final output from a Maven build is usually an enterprise archive, or EAR file for short. This contains Java Enterprise applications.

It is final deployment artifacts such as these that we will later deploy to our production servers.

In this chapter, we concern ourselves with building the artifacts required for deployment, and in *Chapter 7, Deploying the Code*, we talk about the final deployment of our artifacts.

However, even when building our artifacts, we need to understand how to deploy them. At the moment, we will use the following rule of thumb: OS-level packaging is preferable to specialized packaging. This is my personal preference, and others might disagree.

Let's briefly discuss the background for this rule of thumb as well as the alternatives.

As a concrete example, let's consider the deployment of a Java EAR. Normally, we can do this in several ways. Here are some examples:

- Deploy the EAR file as an RPM package through the mechanisms and channels available in the base operating system
- Deploy the EAR through the mechanisms available with the Java application server, such as JBoss, WildFly, and Glassfish

It might superficially look like it would be better to use the mechanism specific to the Java application server to deploy the EAR file, since it is specific to the application server anyway. If Java development is all you ever do, this might be a reasonable supposition. However, since you need to manage your base operating system anyway, you already have methods of deployment available to you that are possible to reuse.

Also, since it is quite likely that you are not just doing Java development but also need to deploy and manage HTML and JavaScript at the very least, it starts to make sense to use a more versatile method of deployment.

Nearly all the organizations I have experience of have had complicated architectures comprising many different technologies, and this rule of thumb has served well in most scenarios.

The only real exception is in mixed environments where Unix servers coexist with Windows servers. In these cases, the Unix servers usually get to use their preferred package distribution method, and the Windows servers have to limp along with some kind of home-brewed solution. This is just an observation and not a condoning of the situation.

Cheating with FPM

Building operating system deliverables such as RPMs with a spec file is very useful knowledge. However, sometimes you don't need the rigor of a real spec file. The spec file is, after all, optimized for the scenario where you are not yourself the originator of the code base.

There is a Ruby-based tool called FPM, which can generate source RPMs suitable for building, directly from the command line.

The tool is available on GitHub at `https://github.com/jordansissel/fpm`.

On Fedora, you can install FPM like this:

```
yum install rubygems
yum install ruby
yum install ruby-devel gcc
gem install fpm
```

This will install a shell script that wraps the FPM Ruby program.

One of the interesting aspects of FPM is that it can generate different types of package; among the supported types are RPM and Debian.

Here is a simple example to make a "hello world" shell script:

```
#!/bin/sh
echo 'Hello World!'
```

We would like the shell script to be installed in /usr/local/bin, so create a directory in your home directory with the following structure:

```
$HOME/hello/usr/local/bin/hello.sh
```

Make the script executable, and then package it:

```
chmod a+x usr/local/bin/hello.sh
fpm -s dir -t rpm -n hello-world -v 1 -C installdir usr
```

This will result in an RPM with the name hello-world and version 1.

To test the package, we can first list the contents and then install it:

```
rpm -qivp hello-world.rpm
rpm -ivh hello-world.rpm
```

The shell script should now be nicely installed in /usr/local/bin.

FPM is a very convenient method for creating RPM, Debian, and other package types. It's a little bit like cheating!

Continuous Integration

The principal benefit of using a build server is achieving Continuous Integration. Each time a change in the code base is detected, a build that tests the quality of the newly submitted code is started.

Since there might be many developers working on the code base, each with slightly different versions, it's important to see whether all the different changes work together properly. This is called **integration testing**. If integration tests are too far apart, there is a growing risk of the different code branches diverging too much, and merging is no longer easy. The result is often referred to as "merge hell". It's no longer clear how a developer's local changes should be merged to the master branch, because of divergence between the branches. This situation is very undesirable. The root cause of merge hell is often, perhaps surprisingly, psychological. There is a mental barrier to overcome in order to merge your changes to the mainline. Part of working with DevOps is making things easier and thus reducing the perceived costs associated with doing important work like submitting changes.

Continuous Integration builds are usually performed in a more stringent manner than what developers do locally. These builds take a longer time to perform, but since performant hardware is not so expensive these days, our build server is beefy enough to cope with these builds.

If the builds are fast enough to not be seen as tedious, developers will be enthused to check in often, and integration problems will be found early.

Continuous Delivery

After the Continuous Integration steps have completed successfully, you have shiny new artifacts that are ready to be deployed to servers. Usually, these are test environments set up to behave like production servers.

We will discuss deployment system alternatives later in the book.

Often, the last thing a build server does is to deploy the final artifacts from the successful build to an artifact repository. From there, the deployment servers take over the responsibility of deploying them to the application servers. In the Java world, the Nexus repository manager is fairly common. It has support for other formats besides the Java formats, such as JavaScript artifacts and Yum channels for RPMs. Nexus also supports the Docker Registry API now.

Using Nexus for RPM distributions is just one option. You can build Yum channels with a shell script fairly easily.

Jenkins plugins

Jenkins has a plugin system to add functionality to the build server. There are many different plugins available, and they can be installed from within the Jenkins web interface. Many of them can be installed without even restarting Jenkins. This screenshot shows a list of some of the available plugins:

Among others, we need the Git plugin to poll our source code repositories.

Our sample organization has opted for Clojure for their build, so we will install the Leingingen plugin.

The host server

The build server is usually a pretty important machine for the organization. Building software is processor as well as memory and disk intensive. Builds shouldn't take too long, so you will need a server with good specifications for the build server — with lots of disk space, processor cores, and RAM.

The build server also has a kind of social aspect: it is here that the code of many different people and roles integrates properly for the first time. This aspect grows in importance if the servers are fast enough. Machines are cheaper than people, so don't let this particular machine be the area you save money on.

Build slaves

To reduce build queues, you can add build slaves. The master server will send builds to the slaves based on a round-robin scheme or tie specific builds to specific build slaves.

The reason for this is usually that some builds have certain requirements on the host operating system.

Build slaves can be used to increase the efficiency of parallel builds. They can also be used to build software on different operating systems. For instance, you can have a Linux Jenkins master server and Windows slaves for components that use Windows build tools. To build software for the Apple Mac, it's useful to have a Mac build slave, especially since Apple has quirky rules regarding the deployment of their operating system on virtual servers.

There are several methods to add build slaves to a Jenkins master; see
https://wiki.jenkins-ci.org/display/JENKINS/Distributed+builds.

In essence, there must be a way for the Jenkins master to issue commands to the build slave. This command channel can be the classic SSH method, and Jenkins has a built-in SSH facility. You can also start a Jenkins slave by downloading a Java JNLP client from the master to the slave. This is useful if the build slave doesn't have an SSH server.

A note on cross-compiling

While it's possible to use Windows build slaves, sometimes it's actually easier to use Linux to build Windows software. C compilers such as GCC can be configured to perform cross-compilation using the MinGW package.

Whether or not this is easier very much depends on the software being built.

A big system usually comprises many different parts, and some of the parts might contain native code for different platforms.

Here are some examples:

- Native android components
- Native server components coded in C for efficiency
- Native client components, also coded in C or C++ for efficiency

The prevalence of native code depends a bit on the nature of the organization you are working with. Telecom products often have a lot of native code, such as codecs and hardware interface code. Banking systems might have high-speed messaging systems in native code.

An aspect of this is that it is important to be able to build all the code that's in use conveniently on the build server. Otherwise, there's a tendency for some code to be only buildable on some machine collecting dust under somebody's desk. This is a risk that needs to be avoided.

What your organization's systems need, only you can tell.

Software on the host

Depending on the complexity of your builds, you might need to install many different types of build tool on your build server. Remember that Jenkins is mostly used to trigger builds, not perform the builds themselves. That job is delegated to the build system used, such as Maven or Make.

In my experience, it's most convenient to have a Linux-based host operating system. Most of the build systems are available in the distribution repositories, so it's very convenient to install them from there.

To keep your build server up to date, you can use the same deployment servers that you use to keep your application servers up to date.

Triggers

You can either use a timer to trigger builds, or you can poll the code repository for changes and build if there were changes.

It can be useful to use both methods at the same time:

- Git repository polling can be used most of the time so that every check in triggers a build.

- Nightly builds can be triggered, which are more stringent than continuous builds, and thus take a longer time. Since these builds happen at night when nobody is supposed to work, it doesn't matter if they are slow.

- An upstream build can trigger a downstream build.

You can also let the successful build of one job trigger another job.

Job chaining and build pipelines

It's often useful to be able to chain jobs together. In its simplest form, this works by triggering a second job in the event that the first job finishes successfully. Several jobs can be cascaded this way in a chain. Such a build chain is quite often good enough for many purposes. Sometimes, a nicer visualization of the build steps as well as greater control over the details of the chain is desired.

In Jenkins terminology, the first build in a chain is called the upstream build, and the second one is called the downstream build.

While this way of chaining builds is often sufficient, there will most likely be a need for greater control of the build chain eventually. Such a build chain is often called a pipeline or workflow.

There are many plugins that create improved pipelines for Jenkins, and the fact that there are several shows that there is indeed a great desire for improvements in this area.

Two examples are the multijob plugin and the workflow plugin.

The workflow plugin is the more advanced and also has the advantage that it can be described in a Groovy DSL rather than fiddling about in a web UI.

The workflow plugin is promoted by CloudBees, who are the principal contributors to Jenkins today.

An example workflow is illustrated here:

When you have a look at the Groovy build script that the workflow plugin uses, you might get the idea that Jenkins is basically a build tool with a web interface, and you would be more or less correct.

A look at the Jenkins filesystem layout

It is often useful to know where builds wind up in the filesystem.

In the case of the Fedora package, the Jenkins jobs are stored here:

```
/var/lib/jenkins/jobs
```

Each job gets its own directory, and the job description XML is stored in this directory as well as a directory for the build called workspace. The job's XML files can be backed up to another server in order to be able to rebuild the Jenkins server in the event of a catastrophic failure. There are dedicated backup plugins for this purpose as well.

Builds can consume a lot of space, so it may sometimes happen that you need to clean out this space manually.

This shouldn't be the normal case, of course. You should configure Jenkins to only leave the number of builds you have space for. You can also configure your configuration management tool to clear out space if needed.

Another reason you might need to delve into the filesystem is when a build mysteriously fails, and you need to debug the cause of the failure. A common cause of this is when the build server state does not meet expectations. For a Maven build, broken dependencies could be polluting the local repository on the build server, for example.

Build servers and infrastructure as code

While we are discussing the Jenkins file structure, it is useful to note an impedance mismatch that often occurs between GUI-based tools such as Jenkins and the DevOps axiom that infrastructure should be described as code.

One way to understand this problem is that while Jenkins job descriptors are text file-based, these text files are not the primary interface for changing the job descriptors. The web interface is the primary interface. This is both a strength and weakness.

It is easy to create ad-hoc solutions on top of existing builds with Jenkins. You don't need to be intimately familiar with Jenkins to do useful work.

On the other hand, the out-of-the-box experience of Jenkins lacks many features that we are used to from the world of programming. Basic features like inheritance and even function definitions take some effort to provide in Jenkins.

The build server feature in GitLab, for example, takes a different approach. Build descriptors are just code right from the start. It is worth checking out this feature in GitLab if you don't need all the possibilities that Jenkins offers.

Building by dependency order

Many build tools have the concept of a build tree where dependencies are built in the order required for the build to complete, since parts of the build might depend on other parts.

In Make-like tools, this is described explicitly; for instance, like this:

```
a.out : b.o c.o
b.o : b.c
c.o : c.c
```

So, in order to build `a.out`, `b.o` and `c.o` must be built first.

In tools such as Maven, the build graph is derived from the dependencies we set for an artifact. Gradle, another Java build tool, also creates a build graph before building.

Jenkins has support for visualizing the build order for Maven builds, which is called the **reactor** in Maven parlance, in the web user interface.

This view is not available for Make-style builds, however.

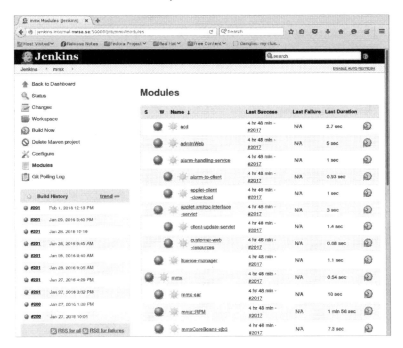

Build phases

One of the principal benefits of the Maven build tool is that it standardizes builds.

This is very useful for a large organization, since it won't need to invent its own build standards. Other build tools are usually much more lax regarding how to implement various build phases. The rigidity of Maven has its pros and cons. Sometimes, people who get started with Maven reminisce about the freedom that could be had with tools such as Ant.

You can implement these build phases with any tool, but it's harder to keep the habit going when the tool itself doesn't enforce the standard order: building, testing, and deploying.

We will examine testing in more detail in a later chapter, but we should note here that the testing phase is very important. The Continuous Integration server needs to be very good at catching errors, and automated testing is very important for achieving that goal.

Alternative build servers

While Jenkins appears to be pretty dominant in the build server scene in my experience, it is by no means alone. Travis CI is a hosted solution that is popular among open source projects. Buildbot is a buildserver that is written in, and configurable with, Python. The Go server is another one, from ThoughtWorks. Bamboo is an offering from Atlassian. GitLab also supports build server functionality now.

Do shop around before deciding on which build server works best for you.

When evaluating different solutions, be aware of attempts at vendor lock-in. Also keep in mind that the build server does not in any way replace the need for builds that are well behaved locally on a developer's machine.

Also, as a common rule of thumb, see if the tool is configurable via configuration files. While management tends to be impressed by graphical configuration, developers and operations personnel rarely like being forced to use a tool that can only be configured via a graphical user interface.

Collating quality measures

A useful thing that a build server can do is the collation of software quality metrics. Jenkins has some support for this out of the box. Java unit tests are executed and can be visualized directly on the job page.

Another more advanced option is using the Sonar code quality visualizer, which is shown in the following screenshot. Sonar tests are run during the build phase and propagated to the Sonar server, where they are stored and visualized.

A Sonar server can be a great way for a development team to see the fruits of their efforts at improving the code base.

The drawback of implementing a Sonar server is that it sometimes slows down the builds. The recommendation is to perform the Sonar builds in your nightly builds, once a day.

About build status visualization

The build server produces a lot of data that is amenable to visualization on a shared display. It is useful to be immediately aware that a build has failed, for instance.

The easiest thing is to just hook up a monitor in a kiosk-like configuration with a web browser pointing to your build server web interface. Jenkins has many plugins that provide a simplified job overview suitable for kiosk displays. These are sometimes called **information radiators**.

It is also common to hook up other types of hardware to the build status, such as lava lamps or colorful LED lamps.

In my experience, this kind of display can make people enthusiastic about the build server. Succeeding with having a useful display in the long run is more tricky than it would first appear, though. The screen can be distracting. If you put the screen where it's not easily seen in order to circumvent the distraction, the purpose of the display is defeated.

A lava lamp in combination with a screen placed discreetly could be a useful combination. The lava lamp is not normally lit, and thus not distracting. When a build error occurs, it lights up, and then you know that you should have a look at the build information radiator. The lava lamp even conveys a form of historical record of the build quality. As the lava lamp lights up, it grows warm, and after a while, the lava moves around inside the lamp. When the error is corrected, the lamp cools down, but the heat remains for a while, so the lava will move around for a time proportional to how long it took to fix the build error.

Taking build errors seriously

The build server can signal errors and code quality problems as much as it wants; if developer teams don't care about the problems, then the investment in the notifications and visualization is all for nought.

This isn't something that can be solved by technical means alone. There has to be a process that everybody agrees on, and the easiest way for a consensus to be achieved is for the process to be of obvious benefit to everyone involved.

Part of the problem is organizations where everything is on fire all the time. Is a build error more important than a production error? If code quality measures estimate that it will take years to improve a code base's quality, is it worthwhile to even get started with fixing the issues?

How do we solve these kinds of problems?

Here are some ideas:

- Don't overdo your code quality metrics. Reduce testing until reports show levels that are fixable. You can add tests again after the initial set of problems is taken care of.

- Define a priority for problems. Fix production issues first. Then fix build errors. Do not submit new code on top of broken code until the issues are resolved.

Robustness

While it is desirable that the build server becomes one of the focal points in your Continuous Delivery pipeline, also consider that the process of building and deployment should not come to a standstill in the event of a breakdown of the build server. For this reason, the builds themselves should be as robust as possible and repeatable on any host.

This is fairly easy for some builds, such as Maven builds. Even so, a Maven build can exhibit any number of flaws that makes it non-portable.

A C-based build can be pretty hard to make portable if one is not so fortunate as to have all build dependencies available in the operating system repositories. Still, robustness is usually worth the effort.

Summary

In this chapter, we took a whirlwind tour through the systems that build our code. We had a look at constructing a Continuous Integration server with Jenkins. We also examined a number of problems that might arise, because the life of a DevOps engineer is always interesting but not always easy.

In the next chapter, we will continue our efforts to produce code of the highest quality by studying how we can integrate testing in our workflow.

6
Testing the Code

If we are going to release our code early and often, we ought to be confident of its quality. Therefore, we need automated regression testing.

In this chapter, some frameworks for software testing are explored, such as **JUnit** for unit testing and **Selenium** for web frontend testing. We will also find out how these tests are run in our Continuous Integration server, Jenkins, thus forming the first part of our Continuous Delivery pipeline.

Testing is very important for software quality, and it's a very large subject in itself.

We will concern ourselves with these topics in this chapter:

- How to make manual testing easier and less error prone
- Various types of testing, such as unit testing, and how to perform them in practice
- Automated system integration testing

We already had a look at how to accumulate test data with Sonar and Jenkins in the previous chapter, and we will continue to delve deeper into this subject.

Manual testing

Even if test automation has larger potential benefits for DevOps than manual testing, manual testing will always be an important part of software development. If nothing else, we will need to perform our tests manually at least once in order to automate them.

Acceptance testing in particular is hard to replace, even though there have been attempts to do so. Software requirement specifications can be terse and hard to understand even for the people developing the features that implement those requirements. In these cases, quality assurance people with their eyes on the ball are invaluable and irreplaceable.

The things that make manual testing easier are the same things that make automated integration testing easier as well, so there is a synergy to achieve between the different testing strategies.

In order to have happy quality assurance personnel, you need to:

- Manage test data, primarily the contents of backend databases, so that tests give the same results when you run them repeatedly
- Be able to make rapid deployments of new code in order to verify bug fixes

Obvious as this may seem, it can be hard in practice. Maybe you have large production databases that can't just be copied to test environments. Maybe they contain end-user data that needs to be protected under law. In these cases, you need to de-identify the data and wash it of any personal details before deploying it to test environments.

Each organization is different, so it is not possible to give generally useful advice in this area other than the KISS rule: "Keep it simple, stupid."

Pros and cons with test automation

When you talk with people, most are enthusiastic about the prospect of test automation. Imagine all the benefits that await us with it:

- Higher software quality
- Higher confidence that the software releases we make will work as intended
- Less of the monotonous tedium of laborious manual testing.

All very good and desirable things!

In practice, though, if you spend time with different organizations with complex multi-tiered products, you will notice people talking about test automation, but you will also notice a suspicious absence of test automation in practice. Why is that?

If you just compile programs and deploy them once they pass compilation, you will likely be in for a bad experience. Software testing is completely necessary for a program to work reliably in the real world. Manual testing is too slow to achieve Continuous Delivery. So, we need test automation to succeed with Continuous Delivery. Therefore, let's further investigate the problem areas surrounding test automation and see if we can figure out what to do to improve the situation:

- Cheap tests have lower value.

  One problem is that the type of test automation that is fairly cheap to produce, unit testing, typically has lower perceived value than other types of testing. Unit testing is still a good type of testing, but manual testing might be perceived as exposing more bugs in practice. It might then feel unnecessary to write unit tests.

- It is difficult to create test cradles that are relevant to automated integration testing.

  While it is not very difficult to write test cradles or test fixtures for unit tests, it tends to get harder as the test cradle becomes more production-like. This can be because of a lack of hardware resources, licensing, manpower, and so on.

- The functionality of programs vary over time and tests must be adjusted accordingly, which takes time and effort.

  This makes it seem as though test automation just makes it harder to write software without providing a perceived benefit.

  This is especially true in organizations where developers don't have a close relationship with the people working with operations, that is, a non DevOps oriented organization. If someone else will have to deal with your crappy code that doesn't really work as intended, there is no real cost involved for the developers. This isn't a healthy relationship. This is the central problem DevOps aims to solve. The DevOps approach bears this repeating rule: help people with different roles work closer together. In organizations like Netflix, an Agile team is entirely responsible for the success, maintenance, and outages of their service.

- It is difficult to write robust tests that work reliably in many different build scenarios.

  A consequence of this is that developers tend to disable tests in their local builds so that they can work undisturbed with the feature they have been assigned. Since people don't work with the tests, changes that affect the test outcomes creep in, and eventually, the tests fail.

The build server will pick up the build error, but nobody remembers how the test works now, and it might take several days to fix the test error. While the test is broken, the build displays will show red, and eventually, people will stop caring about build issues. Someone else will fix the problem eventually.

- It is just hard to write good automated tests, period.

  It can indeed be hard to create good automated integration tests. It can also be rewarding, because you get to learn all the aspects of the system you are testing.

  These are all difficult problems, especially since they mostly stem from people's perceptions and relationships.

There is no panacea, but I suggest adopting the following strategy:

- Leverage people's enthusiasm regarding test automation
- Don't set unrealistic goals
- Work incrementally

Unit testing

Unit testing is the sort of testing that is normally close at heart for developers. The primary reason is that, by definition, unit testing tests well-defined parts of the system in isolation from other parts. Thus, they are comparatively easy to write and use.

Many build systems have built-in support for unit tests, which can be leveraged without undue difficulty.

With Maven, for example, there is a convention that describes how to write tests such that the build system can find them, execute them, and finally prepare a report of the outcome. Writing tests basically boils down to writing test methods, which are tagged with source code annotations to mark the methods as being tests. Since they are ordinary methods, they can do anything, but by convention, the tests should be written so that they don't require considerable effort to run. If the test code starts to require complicated setup and runtime dependencies, we are no longer dealing with unit tests.

Here, the difference between unit testing and functional testing can be a source of confusion. Often, the same underlying technologies and libraries are reused between unit and functional testing.

This is a good thing as reuse is good in general and lets you benefit from your expertise in one area as you work on another. Still, it can be confusing at times, and it pays to raise your eyes now and then to see that you are doing the right thing.

JUnit in general and JUnit in particular

You need something that runs your tests. JUnit is a framework that lets you define unit tests in your Java code and run them.

JUnit belongs to a family of testing frameworks collectively called **xUnit**. The **SUnit** is the grandfather of this family and was designed by Kent Beck in 1998 for the Smalltalk language.

While JUnit is specific to Java, the ideas are sufficiently generic for ports to have been made in, for instance, C#. The corresponding test framework for C# is called, somewhat unimaginatively, **NUnit**. The N is derived from .NET, the name of the Microsoft software platform.

We need some of the following nomenclature before carrying on. The nomenclature is not specific to JUnit, but we will use JUnit as an example to make it easier to relate to the definitions.

- **Test runner:** A test runner runs tests that are defined by an xUnit framework.

    JUnit has a way to run unit tests from the command line, and Maven employs a test runner called Surefire. A test runner also collects and reports test results. In the case of Surefire, the reports are in XML format, and these reports can be further processed by other tools, particularly for visualization.

- **Test case:** A test case is the most fundamental type of test definition.

    How you create test cases differs a little bit among JUnit versions. In earlier versions, you inherited from a JUnit base class; in recent versions, you just need to annotate the test methods. This is better since Java doesn't support multiple inheritance and you might want to use your own inheritance hierarchies rather than the JUnit ones. By convention, Surefire also locates test classes that have the `Test` suffix in the class name.

- **Test fixtures:** A test fixture is a known state that the test cases can rely on so that the tests can have well-defined behavior. It is the responsibility of the developer to create these. A test fixture is also sometimes known as a test context.

With JUnit, you usually use the `@Before` and `@After` annotations to define test fixtures. `@Before` is, unsurprisingly, run before a test case and is used to bring up the environment. `@After` likewise restores the state if there is a need to.

Sometimes, `@Before` and `@After` are more descriptively named **Setup** and **Teardown**. Since annotations are used, the method can have the names that are the most intuitive in that context.

- **Test suites:** You can group test cases together in test suites. A test suite is usually a set of test cases that share the same test fixture.

- **Test execution:** A test execution runs the tests suites and test cases.

  Here, all the previous aspects are combined. The test suites and test cases are located, the appropriate test fixtures are created, and the test cases run. Lastly, the test results are collected and collated.

- **Test result formatter:** A test result formatter formats test result output for human consumption. The format employed by JUnit is versatile enough to be used by other testing frameworks and formatters not directly associated with JUnit. So, if you have some tests that don't really use any of the xUnit frameworks, you can still benefit by presenting the test results in Jenkins by providing a test result XML file. Since the file format is XML, you can produce it from your own tool, if need be.

- **Assertions:** An assertion is a construct in the xUnit framework that makes sure that a condition is met. If it is not met, it is considered an error, and a test error is reported. The test case is also usually terminated when the assertion fails.

JUnit has a number of assertion methods available. Here is a sample of the available assertion methods:

- To check whether two objects are equal:

  ```
  assertEquals(str1, str2);
  ```

- To check whether a condition is true:

  ```
  assertTrue (val1 < val2);
  ```

- To check whether a condition is false:

  ```
  assertFalse(val1 > val2);
  ```

A JUnit example

JUnit is well supported by Java build tools. It will serve well as an example of JUnit testing frameworks in general.

If we use Maven, by convention, it will expect to find test cases in the following directory:

```
/src/test/java
```

Mocking

Mocking refers to the practice of writing simulated resources to enable unit testing. Sometimes, the words "fake" or "stub" are used. For example, a middleware system that responds with JSON structures from a database would "mock" the database backend for its unit tests. Otherwise, the unit tests would require the database backend to be online, probably also requiring exclusive access. This wouldn't be convenient.

Mockito is a mocking framework for Java that has also been ported to Python.

Test Coverage

When you hear people talk about unit testing, they often talk about test coverage. Test coverage is the percentage of the application code base that is actually executed by the test cases.

In order to measure unit test code coverage, you need to execute the tests and keep track of the code that has or hasn't been executed.

Cobertura is a test coverage measurement utility for Java that does this. Other such utilities include jcoverage and Clover.

Cobertura works by instrumenting the Java bytecode, inserting code fragments of its own into already compiled code. These code fragments are executed while measuring code coverage during execution of test cases

Its usually assumed that a hundred percent test coverage is the ideal. This might not always be the case, and one should be aware of the cost/benefit trade-offs.

A simple counterexample is a simple getter method in Java:

```
private int positiveValue;
void setPositiveValue(int x){
  this.positiveValue=x;
}

int getPositiveValue(){
  return positiveValue;
}
```

If we write a test case for this method, we will achieve a higher test coverage. On the other hand, we haven't achieved much of anything, in practice. The only thing we are really testing is that our Java implementation doesn't have bugs.

If, on the other hand, the setter is changed to include validation to check that the value is not a negative number, the situation changes. As soon as a method includes logic of some kind, unit testing is useful.

Automated integration testing

Automated integration testing is similar in many ways to unit testing with respect to the basic techniques that are used. You can use the same test runners and build system support. The primary difference with unit testing is that less mocking is involved.

Where a unit test would simply mock the data returned from a backend database, an integration test would use a real database for its tests. A database is a decent example of the kind of testing resources you need and what types of problems they could present.

Automated integration testing can be quite tricky, and you need to be careful with your choices.

If you are testing, say, a read-only middleware adapter, such as a SOAP adapter for a database, it might be possible to use a production database copy for your testing. You need the database contents to be predictable and repeatable; otherwise, it will be hard to write and run your tests.

The added value here is that we are using a production data copy. It might contain data that is hard to predict if you were to create test data from scratch. The requirements are the same as for manual testing. With automated integration testing, you need, well, more automation than with manual testing. For databases, this doesn't have to be very complicated. Automated database backup and restore are well-known operations.

Docker in automated testing

Docker can be quite convenient when building automated test rigs. It adds some of the features of unit testing but at a functional level. If your application consists of several server components in a cluster, you can simulate the entire cluster with a set of containers. Docker provides a virtual network for the cluster that makes clear how the containers interact at the network level.

Docker also makes it easy to restore a container to a known state. If you have your test database in a Docker container, you can easily restore the database to the same state as before the tests taking place. This is similar to restoring the environment in the `After` method in unit tests.

The Jenkins Continuous Integration server has support for the starting and stopping of containers, which can be useful when working with Docker test automation.

Using Docker Compose to run the containers you need is also a useful option.

Docker is still young, and some aspects of using Docker for test automation can require glue code that is less than elegant.

A simple example could be firing up a database container and an application server container that communicate with each other. The basic process of starting the containers is simple and can be done with a shell script or Docker Compose. But, since we want to run tests on the application server container that has been started, how do we know whether it was properly started? In the case of the WildFly container, there is no obvious way to determine the running state apart from watching the log output for occurrences of strings or maybe polling a web socket. In any case, these types of hacks are not very elegant and are time consuming to write. The end result can be well worth the effort, though.

Arquillian

Arquillian is an example of a test tool that allows a level of testing closer to integration testing than unit testing together with mocking allows. Arquillian is specific to Java application servers such as WildFly. Arquillian is interesting because it illustrates the struggle of reaching a closer approximation of production systems during testing. You can reach such approximations in any number of ways, and the road to there is filled with trade-offs.

There is a "hello world" style demonstration of Arquillian in the book's source code archive.

Performance testing

Performance testing is an essential part of the development of, for instance, large public web sites.

Performance testing presents similar challenges as integration testing. We need a testing system that is similar to a production system in order for the performance test data to be useful to make a forecast about real production system performance.

The most commonly used performance test is load testing. With load testing, we measure, among other things, the response time of a server while the performance testing software generates synthetic requests for the server.

Apache JMeter is an example of a an open source application for measuring performance. While it's simpler than its proprietary counterparts, such as LoadRunner, JMeter is quite useful, and simplicity is not really a bad thing.

JMeter can generate simulated load and measure response times for a number of protocols, such as HT, LDAP, SOAP, and JDBC.

There is a JMeter Maven plugin, so you can run JMeter as part of your build.

JMeter can also be used in a Continuous Integration server. There is a plugin for Jenkins, called the performance plugin, that can execute JMeter test scenarios.

Ideally, the Continuous Integration server will deploy code that has been built to a test environment that is production-like. After deployment, the performance tests will be executed and test data collected, as shown in this screenshot:

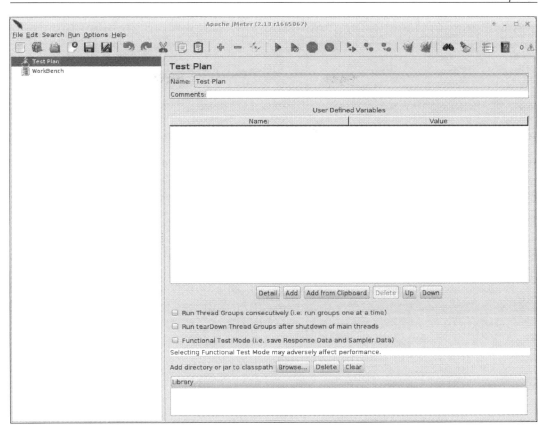

Automated acceptance testing

Automated acceptance testing is a method of ensuring that your testing is valid from the end user's point of view.

Cucumber is a framework where test cases are written in plaintext and associated with test code. This is called **behavior-driven development**. The original implementation of Cucumber was written in Ruby, but ports now exist for many different languages.

The appeal of Cucumber from a DevOps point of view is that it is intended to bring different roles together. Cucumber feature definitions are written in a conversational style that can be achieved without programming skills. The hard data required for test runs is then extracted from the descriptions and used for the tests.

While the intentions are good, there are difficulties in implementing Cucumber that might not immediately be apparent. While the language of the behavior specifications is basically free text, they still need to be somewhat spartan and formalized; otherwise, it becomes difficult to write matching code that extracts the test data from the descriptions. This makes writing the specifications less attractive to the roles that were supposed to write them in the first place. What then happens is that programmers write the specifications, and they often dislike the verbosity and resort to writing ordinary unit tests.

As with many things, cooperation is of the essence here. Cucumber can work great when developers and product owners work together on writing the specifications in a way that works for everyone concerned.

Now, let's look at a small "hello world" style example for Cucumber.

Cucumber works with plaintext files called feature files, which look like this:

```
Feature: Addition
    I would like to add numbers with my pocket calculator

    Scenario: Integer numbers
      * I have entered 4 into the calculator
      * I press add
      * I have entered 2 into the calculator
      * I press equal
      * The result should be 6 on the screen
```

The feature description is implementation-language neutral. Describing the Cucumber test code is done in a vocabulary called **Gherkin**.

If you use the Java 8 lambda version of Cucumber, a test step could look somewhat like this:

```
Calculator calc;
public MyStepdefs() {
  Given("I have entered (\\d+) into the calculator", (Integer i) -> {
    System.out.format("Number entered: %n\n", i);
    calc.push(i);
  });
```

```
When("I press (\\w+)", (String op) -> {
  System.out.format("operator entered: %n\n", op);
  calc.op(op);
});
Then("The result should be (\\d+)", (Integer i) -> {
  System.out.format("result : %n\n", i);
  assertThat(calc.result(),i);
});
```

The complete code can, as usual, be found in the book's source archive.

This is a simple example, but it should immediately be apparent both what the strengths and weaknesses with Cucumber are. The feature descriptions have a nice human-readable flair. However, you have to match the strings with regular expressions in your test code. If your feature description changes even slightly in wording, you will have to adjust the test code.

Automated GUI testing

Automating GUI testing has many desirable properties, but it is also difficult. One reason is that user interfaces tend to change a lot during the development phase, and buttons and controls move around in the GUI.

Older generations of GUI testing tools often worked by synthesizing mouse events and sending them to the GUI. When a button moved, the simulated mouse click went nowhere, and the test failed. It then became expensive to keep the tests updated with changes in the GUI.

Selenium is a web UI testing toolkit that uses a different, more effective, approach. The controllers are instrumented with identifiers so that Selenium can find the controllers by examining the document object model (DOM) rather than blindly generating mouse clicks.

Selenium works pretty well in practice and has evolved over the years.

Another method is employed by the Sikuli test framework. It uses a computer vision framework, OpenCV, to help identify controllers even if they move or change appearances. This is useful for testing native applications, such as games.

The screenshot included below is from the Selenium IDE.

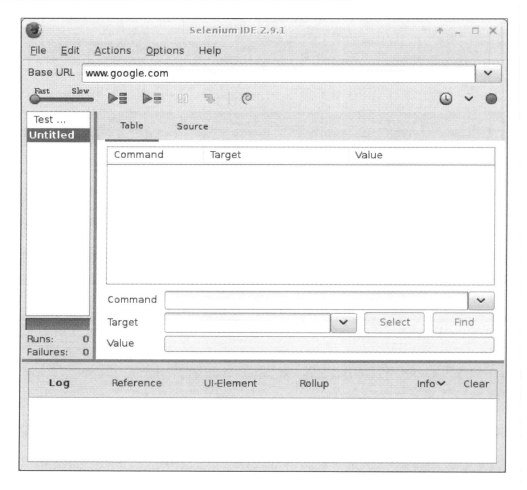

Integrating Selenium tests in Jenkins

Selenium works by invoking a browser, pointing it to a web server running your application, and then remotely controlling the browser by integrating itself in the JavaScript and DOM layers.

When you develop the tests, you can use two basic methods:

- Record user interactions in the browser and later save the resulting test code for reuse
- Write the tests from scratch using Selenium's test API

Many developers prefer to write tests as code using the Selenium API at the outset, which can be combined with a test-driven development approach.

Regardless of how the tests are developed, they need to run in the integration build server.

This means that you need browsers installed somewhere in your test environment. This can be a bit problematic since build servers are usually headless, that is, they are servers that don't run user interfaces.

It's possible to wrap a browser in a simulated desktop environment on the build server.

A more advanced solution is using Selenium Grid. As the name implies, Selenium Grid provides a server that gives a number of browser instances that can be used by the tests. This makes it possible to run a number of tests in parallel as well as to provide a set of different browser configurations.

You can start out with the single browser solution and later migrate to the Selenium Grid solution when you need it.

There is also a convenient Docker container that implements Selenium Grid.

JavaScript testing

Since there usually are web UI implementations of nearly every product these days, the JavaScript testing frameworks deserve special mention:

- Karma is a test runner for unit tests in the JavaScript language
- Jasmine is a Cucumber-like behavior testing framework
- Protractor is used for AngularJS

Protractor is a different testing framework, similar to Selenium in scope but optimized for AngularJS, a popular JavaScript user interface framework. While it would appear that new web development frameworks come and go everyday, it's interesting to note why a test framework like Protractor exists when Selenium is available and is general enough to test AngularJS applications too.

First of all, Protractor actually uses the Selenium web driver implementation under the hood.

You can write Protractor tests in JavaScript, but you can use JavaScript for writing test cases for Selenium as well if you don't like writing them in a language like Java.

The main benefit turns out to be that Protractor has internalized knowledge about the Angular framework, which a general framework like Selenium can't really have.

AngularJS has a model/view setup that is particular to it. Other frameworks use other setups, since the model/view setup isn't something that is intrinsic to the JavaScript language—not yet, anyway.

Protractor knows about the peculiarities of Angular, so it's easier to locate controllers in the testing code with special constructs.

Testing backend integration points

Automated testing of backend functionality such as SOAP and REST endpoints is normally quite cost effective. Backend interfaces tend to be fairly stable, so the corresponding tests will also require less maintenance effort than GUI tests, for instance.

The tests can also be fairly easy to write with tools such as soapUI, which can be used to write and execute tests. These tests can also be run from the command line and with Maven, which is great for Continuous Integration on a build server.

The soapUI is a good example of a tool that appeals to several different roles. Testers who build test cases get a fairly well-structured environment for writing tests and running them interactively. Tests can be built incrementally.

Developers can integrate test cases in their builds without necessarily using the GUI. There are Maven plugins and command-line runners.

The command line and Maven integration are useful for people maintaining the build server too.

Furthermore, the licensing is open source with some added features in a separate, proprietary version. The open source nature makes the builds more reliable. It is very stress-inducing when a build fails because a license has unexpectedly reached its end or a floating license has run out.

The soapUI tool has its share of flaws, but in general, it is flexible and works well. Here's what the user interface looks like:

The soapUI user interface is fairly straightforward. There is a tree view listing test cases on the left. It is possible to select single tests or entire test suites and run them. The results are presented in the area on the right.

It is also worth noting that the test cases are defined in XML. This makes it possible to manage them as code in the source code repository. This also makes it possible to edit them in a text editor on occasion, for instance, when we need to perform a global search and replace on an identifier that has changed names—just the way we like it in DevOps!

Test-driven development

Test-driven development (TDD) has an added focus on test automation. It was made popular by the Extreme programming movement of the nineties.

TDD is usually described as a sequence of events, as follows:

- **Implement the test**: As the name implies, you start out by writing the test and write the code afterwards. One way to see it is that you implement the interface specifications of the code to be developed and then progress by writing the code. To be able to write the test, the developer must find all relevant requirement specifications, use cases, and user stories.

  The shift in focus from coding to understanding the requirements can be beneficial for implementing them correctly.

- **Verify that the new test fails**: The newly added test should fail because there is nothing to implement the behavior properly yet, only the stubs and interfaces needed to write the test. Run the test and verify that it fails.

- **Write code that implements the tested feature**: The code we write doesn't yet have to be particularly elegant or efficient. Initially, we just want to make the new test pass.

- **Verify that the new test passes together with the old tests:** When the new test passes, we know that we have implemented the new feature correctly. Since the old tests also pass, we haven't broken existing functionality.

- **Refactor the code:** The word "refactor" has mathematical roots. In programming, it means cleaning up the code and, among other things, making it easier to understand and maintain. We need to refactor since we cheated a bit earlier in the development.

TDD is a style of development that fits well with DevOps, but it's not necessarily the only one. The primary benefit is that you get good test suites that can be used in Continuous Integration tests.

REPL-driven development

While REPL-driven development isn't a widely recognized term, it is my favored style of development and has a particular bearing on testing. This style of development is very common when working with interpreted languages, such as Lisp, Python, Ruby, and JavaScript.

When you work with a Read Eval Print Loop (REPL), you write small functions that are independent and also not dependent on a global state.

The functions are tested even as you write them.

This style of development differs a bit from TDD. The focus is on writing small functions with no or very few side effects. This makes the code easy to comprehend rather than when writing test cases before functioning code is written, as in TDD.

You can combine this style of development with unit testing. Since you can use REPL-driven development to develop your tests as well, this combination is a very effective strategy.

A complete test automation scenario

We have looked at a number of different ways of working with test automation. Assembling the pieces into a cohesive whole can be daunting.

In this section, we will have a look at a complete test automation example, continuing from the user database web application for our organization, Matangle.

You can find the source code in the accompanying source code bundle for the book.

The application consists of the following layers:

- A web frontend
- A JSON/REST service interface
- An application backend layer
- A database layer

The test code will work through the following phases during execution:

- Unit testing of the backend code
- Functional testing of the web frontend, performed with the Selenium web testing framework
- Functional testing of the JSON/REST interface, executed with soapUI

All the tests are run in sequence, and when all of them succeed, the result can be used as the basis for a decision to see whether the application stack is deemed healthy enough to deploy to a test environment, where manual testing can commence.

Manually testing our web application

Before we can automate something usefully, we need to understand the details of what we will be automating. We need some form of a test plan.

Below, we have a test plan for our web application. It details the steps that a human tester needs to perform by hand if no test automation is available. It is similar to what a real test plan would look like, except a real plan would normally have many more formalities surrounding it. In our case, we will go directly to the details of the test in question:

1. Start a fresh test. This resets the database backend to a known state and sets up the testing scenario so that manual testing can proceed from a known state.

   The tester points a browser to the application's starting URL:

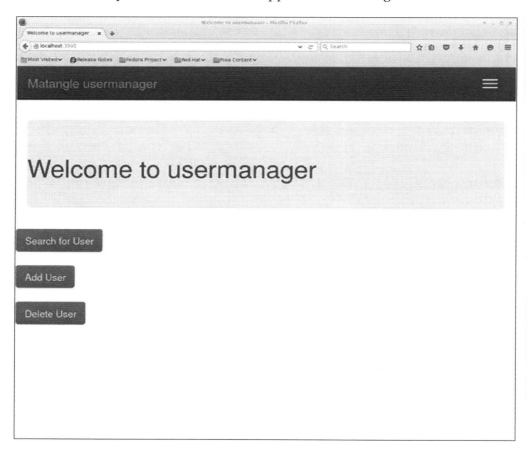

2. Click on the **Add User** link.

3. Add a user:

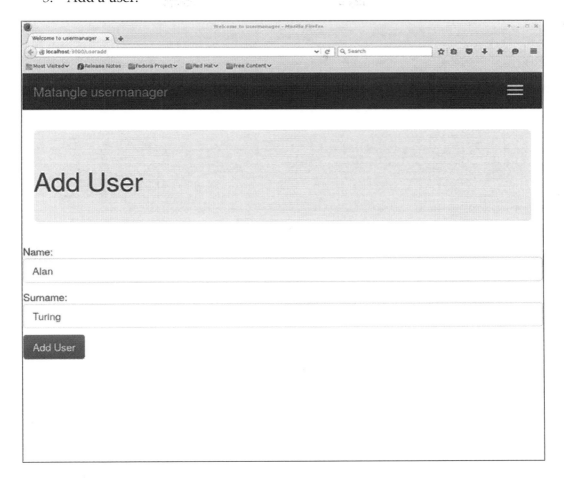

Enter a username—Alan Turing, in our test case.

4. Save the new user. A success page will be shown.

5. Verify that the user was added properly by performing a search:

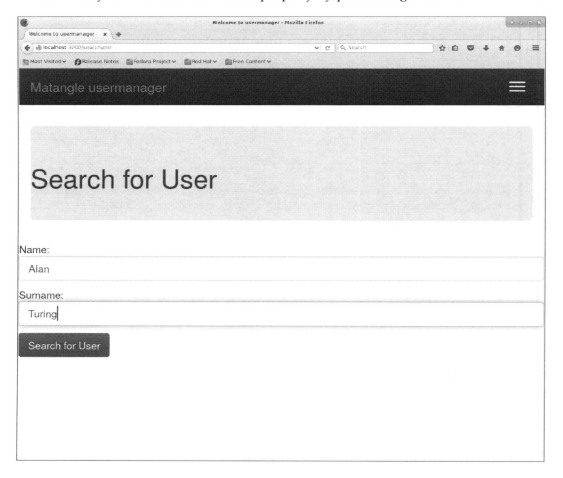

Click on the **Search User** link. Search for **Alan Turing**. Verify that **Alan** is present in the result list.

While the reader is probably less than impressed with the application's complexity at this point, this is the level of detail we need to work with if we are going to be able to automate the scenario, and it is this complexity that we are studying here.

Running the automated test

The test is available in a number of flavors in the source bundle.

To run the first one, you need a Firefox installation.

Choose the one called `autotest_v1`, and run it from the command line:

```
autotest_v1/bin/autotest.sh
```

If all goes well, you will see a Firefox window open, and the test you previously performed by hand will be done automatically. The values you filled in and the links you clicked on by hand will all be automated.

This isn't foolproof yet, because maybe the Firefox version you installed isn't compatible, or something else is amiss with the dependencies. The natural reaction to problems like these is dependency management, and we will look at a variant of dependency management using Docker shortly.

Finding a bug

Now we will introduce a bug and let the test automation system find it.

As an exercise, find the string "Turing" in the test sources. Change one of the occurrences to "Tring" or some other typographical error. Just change one; otherwise, the verification code will believe there is no error and that everything is alright!

Run the tests again, and notice that the error is found by the automatic test system.

Test walkthrough

Now we have run the tests and verified that they work. We have also verified that they are able to discover the bug we created.

What does the implementation look like? There is a lot of code, and it would not be useful to reprint it in the book. It is useful, though, to give an overview of the code and have a look at some snippets of the code.

Open the `autotest_v1/test/pom.xml` file. It's a Maven project object model file, and it's here that all the plugins used by the tests are set up. Maven POM files are declarative XML files and the test steps are step-by-step imperative instructions, so in the latter case, Java is used.

There's a property block at the top, where dependency versions are kept. There is no real need to break out the versions; it has been used in this case to make the rest of the POM file less version-dependent:

```
<properties>
  <junit.version>XXX</junit.version>
  <selenium.version>XXX</selenium.version>
  <cucumber.version>XXX</cucumber.version>
  ...
</properties>
```

Here are the dependencies for JUnit, Selenium and Cucumber:

```
<dependency>
    <groupId>junit</groupId>
    <artifactId>junit</artifactId>
    <version>${junit.version}</version>
</dependency>

<dependency>
    <groupId>org.seleniumhq.selenium</groupId>
    <artifactId>selenium-java</artifactId>
    <version>${selenium.version}</version>
</dependency>

<dependency>
    <groupId>info.cukes</groupId>
    <artifactId>cucumber-core</artifactId>
    <version>${cucumber.version}</version>
</dependency>

<dependency>
    <groupId>info.cukes</groupId>
    <artifactId>cucumber-java</artifactId>
    <version>${cucumber.version}</version>
</dependency>

<dependency>
    <groupId>info.cukes</groupId>
    <artifactId>cucumber-junit</artifactId>
    <version>${cucumber.version}</version>
</dependency>
```

To define the tests according to the Cucumber method, we need a feature file that describes the test steps in a human-readable language. This feature file corresponds to our previous test plan for manual tests:

```
Feature: Manage users
  As an Administrator
  I want to be able to
  - Create a user
  - Search for the user
  - Delete the user

  Scenario: Create a named user
      Given a user with the name 'Alan'
      And the surname 'Turing'
      When the administrator clicks 'Add User'
      Then the user should be added

  Scenario: Search for a named user
      Given a user with the name 'Alan'
      And the surname 'Turing'
      When the administrator clicks 'Search for User'
      Then the user 'Alan Turing' should be shown

  Scenario: Delete a named user
      Given a user with the name 'Alan'
      And the surname 'Turing'
      When the administrator clicks 'Delete User'
      Then the user should be deleted
```

The feature file is mostly plaintext with small elements of machine-readable markup. It's up to the corresponding test code to parse the plaintext of the scenarios with regexes.

It is also possible to localize the feature files to the language used within your own team. This can be useful since the feature files might be written by people who are not accustomed to English.

The feature needs actual concrete code to execute, so you need some way to bind the feature to the code.

You need a test class with some annotations to make Cucumber and JUnit work together:

```
@RunWith(Cucumber.class)
@Cucumber.Options(
        glue = "matangle.glue.manageUser",
        features = "features/manageUser.feature",
        format = {"pretty", "html:target/Cucumber"}
)
```

In this example, the names of the Cucumber test classes have, by convention, a Step suffix.

Now, you need to bind the test methods to the feature scenarios and need some way to pick out the arguments to the test methods from the feature description. With the Java Cucumber implementation, this is mostly done with Java annotations. These annotations correspond to the keywords used in the feature file:

```
@Given(".+a user with the name '(.+)'")
    public void addUser(String name) {
```

In this case, the different inputs are stored in member variables until the entire user interface transaction is ready to go. The sequence of operations is determined by the order in which they appear in the feature file.

To illustrate that Cucumber can have different implementations, there is also a Clojure example in the book's source code bundle.

So far, we have seen that we need a couple of libraries for Selenium and Cucumber to run the tests and how the Cucumber feature descriptor is bound to methods in our test code classes.

The next step is to examine how Cucumber tests execute Selenium test code.

Cucumber test steps mostly call classes with Selenium implementation details in classes with a View suffix. This isn't a technical necessity, but it makes the test step classes more readable, since the particulars of the Selenium framework are kept in a separate class.

The Selenium framework takes care of the communication between the test code and the browser. View classes are an abstraction of the web page that we are automating. There are member variables in the view code that correspond to HTML controllers. You can describe the binding between test code member variables and HTML elements with annotations from the Selenium framework, as follows:

```
@FindBy(id = "name") private WebElement nameInput;
@FindBy(id = "surname") private WebElement surnameInput;
```

The member variable is then used by the test code to automate the same steps that the human tester followed using the test plan. The partitioning of classes into view and step classes also makes the similarity of the step classes to a test plan more apparent. This separation of concerns is useful when people involved with testing and quality assurance work with the code.

To send a string, you use a method to simulate a user typing on a keyboard:

```
nameInput.clear();
nameInput.sendKeys(value);
```

There are a number of useful methods, such as `click()`, which will simulate a user clicking on the control.

Handling tricky dependencies with Docker

Because we used Maven in our test code example, it handled all code dependencies except the browser. While you could clearly deploy a browser such as Firefox to a Maven-compatible repository and handle the test dependency that way if you put your mind to it, this is normally not the way this issue is handled in the case of browsers. Browsers are finicky creatures and show wildly differing behavior in different versions. We need a mechanism to run many different browsers of many different versions.

Luckily, there is such a mechanism, called Selenium Grid. Since Selenium has a pluggable driver architecture, you can essentially layer the browser backend in a client server architecture.

To use Selenium Grid, you must first determine how you want the server part to run. While the easiest option would be to use an online provider, for didactic reasons, it is not the option we will explore here.

There is an `autotest_seleniumgrid` directory, which contains a wrapper to run the test using Docker in order to start a local Selenium Grid. You can try out the example by running the wrapper.

The latest information regarding how to run Selenium Grid is available on the project's GitHub page.

Selenium Grid has a layered architecture, and to set it up, you need three parts:

- A `RemoteWebDriver` instance in your testing code. This will be the interface to Selenium Grid.
- Selenium Hub, which can be seen as a proxy for browser instances.

- Firefox or Chrome grid nodes. These are the browser instances that will be proxied by Hub.

The code to set up the `RemoteWebDriver` could look like this:

```
DesiredCapabilities capabilities = new DesiredCapabilities();
capabilities.setPlatform(Platform.LINUX);
capabilities.setBrowserName("Firefox");
        capabilities.setVersion("35");
    driver = new RemoteWebDriver(
                new URL("http://localhost:4444"),
                capabilities);
```

The code asks for a browser instance with a particular set of capabilities. The system will do its best to oblige.

The code can only work if there is a Selenium Grid Hub running with a Firefox node attached.

Here is how you start Selenium Hub using its Docker packaging:

```
docker run -d -p 4444:4444 --name selenium-hub selenium/hub
```

And here is how you can start a Firefox node and attach it to Hub:

```
docker run -d --link selenium-hub:hub selenium/node-firefox
```

Summary

This concludes the test code walkthrough. When you read the code, you might want to use only a subset of the ideas that are illustrated. Maybe the Cucumber method isn't really a good fit for you, or you value concise and succinct code over the layered abstractions used in the example. That is a natural and sound reaction. Adopt the ideas so they work for your team. Also, have a look at the other flavors of the testing code available in the source bundle when deciding on what works for you!

Software testing is a vast subject that can fill volumes. In this chapter, we surveyed some of the many different types of testing available. We also looked at concrete ways of working with automated software testing in a Continuous Integration server. We used Jenkins and Maven as well as JUnit and JMeter. Although these tools are Java oriented, the concepts translate readily to other environments.

Now that we have built and tested our code, we will start working with deploying our code in the next chapter.

7
Deploying the Code

Now that the code has been built and tested, we need to deploy it to our servers so that our customers can use the newly developed features!

There are many competing tools and options in this space, and the one that is right for you and your organization will depend on your needs.

We will explore Puppet, Ansible, Salt, PalletOps, and others, by showing how to deploy sample applications in different scenarios. Any one of these tools has a vast ecosystem of complementing services and tools, so it is no easy subject to get a grip on.

Throughout the book, we have encountered aspects of some of the different deployment systems that already exist. We had a look at RPMs and .deb files and how to build them with the fpm command. We had a look at various Java artifacts and how Maven uses the idea of a binary repository where you can deploy your versioned artifacts.

In this chapter, we will focus on installing binary packages and their configuration with a configuration management system.

Why are there so many deployment systems?

There is a bewildering abundance of options regarding the installation of packages and configuring them on actual servers, not to mention all the ways to deploy client-side code.

Let's first examine the basics of the problem we are trying to solve.

We have a typical enterprise application, with a number of different high-level components. We don't need to make the scenario overly complex in order to start reasoning about the challenges that exist in this space.

In our scenario, we have:

- A web server
- An application server
- A database server

If we only have a single physical server and these few components to worry about that get released once a year or so, we can install the software manually and be done with the task. It will be the most cost-effective way of dealing with the situation, even though manual work is boring and error prone.

It's not reasonable to expect a conformity to this simplified release cycle in reality though. It is more likely that a large organization has hundreds of servers and applications and that they are all deployed differently, with different requirements.

Managing all the complexity that the real world displays is hard, so it starts to make sense that there are a lot of different solutions that do basically the same thing in different ways.

Whatever the fundamental unit that executes our code is, be it a physical server, a virtual machine, some form of container technology, or a combination of these, we have several challenges to deal with. We will look at them now.

Configuring the base OS

The configuration of the base operating system must be dealt with somehow.

Often, our application stack has subtle, or not so subtle, requirements on the base operating system. Some application stacks, such as Java, Python, or Ruby, make these operating system requirements less apparent, because these technologies go to a great length to offer cross-platform functionality. At other times, the operating system requirements are apparent to a greater degree, such as when you work with low-level mixed hardware and software integrations, which is common in the telecom industry.

There are many existing solutions that deal with this fundamental issue. Some systems work with a bare metal (or bare virtual machine) approach, where they install the desired operating system from scratch and then install all the base dependencies that the organization needs for their servers. Such systems include, for example, Red Hat Satellite and Cobbler, which works in a similar way but is more lightweight.

Cobbler allows you to boot a physical or virtual machine over the network using dhcpd. The DHCP server can then allow you to provide a netboot-compliant image. When the netboot image is started, it contacts Cobbler to retrieve the packages that will be installed in order to create the new operating system. Which packages are installed can be decided on the server from the target machine's network MAC address for instance.

Another method that is very popular today is to provide base operating system images that can be reused between machines. Cloud systems such as AWS, Azure, or OpenStack work this way. When you ask the cloud system for a new virtual machine, it is created using an existing image as a base. Container systems such as Docker also work in a similar way, where you declare your base container image and then describe the changes you want to formulate for your own image.

Describing clusters

There must be a way to describe clusters.

If your organization only has a single machine with a single application, then you might not need to describe how a cluster deployment of your application would look like. Unfortunately (or fortunately, depending on your outlook), the reality is normally that your applications are spread out over a set of machines, virtual or physical.

All the systems we work with in this chapter support this idea in different ways. Puppet has an extensive system that allows machines to have different roles that in turn imply a set of packages and configurations. Ansible and Salt have these systems as well. The container-based Docker system has an emerging infrastructure for describing sets of containers connected together and Docker hosts that can accept and deploy such cluster descriptors.

Cloud systems such as AWS also have methods and descriptors for cluster deployments.

Cluster descriptors are normally also used to describe the application layer.

Delivering packages to a system

There must be a way to deliver packages to a system.

Much of an application can be installed as packages, which are installed unmodified on the target system by the configuration management system. Package systems such as RPM and deb have useful features, such as verifying that the files provided by a package are not tampered with on a target system, by providing checksums for all files in the package. This is useful for security reasons as well as debugging purposes. Package delivery is usually done with operating system facilities such as yum package channels on Red Hat based systems, but sometimes, the configuration management system can also deliver packages and files with its own facilities. These facilities are often used in tandem with the operating system's package channels.

There must be a way to manage configurations that is independent of installed packages.

The configuration management system should, obviously, be able to manage our applications' configurations. This is complex because configuration methods vary wildly between applications, regardless of the many efforts that have been made to unify the field.

The most common and flexible system to configure applications relies on text-based configuration files. There are several other methods, such as using an application that provides an API to handle configuration (such as a command-line interface) or sometimes handling configuration via database settings.

In my experience, configuration systems based on text files create the least amount of hassle and should be preferred for in-house code at least. There are many ways to manage text-based configurations. You can manage them in source code handling systems such as Git. There's a host of tools that can ease the debugging of broken configuration, such as diff. If you are in a tight spot, you can edit configurations directly on the servers using a remote text editor such as Emacs or Vi.

Handling configurations via databases is much less flexible. This is arguably an anti-pattern that usually occurs in organizations where the psychological rift between developer teams and operations teams are too wide, which is something we aim to solve with DevOps. Handling configurations in databases makes the application stack harder to get running. You need a working database to even start the application.

Managing configuration settings via imperative command-line APIs is also a dubious practice for similar reasons but can sometimes be helpful, especially if the API is used to manage an underlying text-based configuration. Many of the configuration management systems, such as Puppet, depend on being able to manage declarative configurations. If we manage the configuration state via other mechanisms, such as command-line imperative API, Puppet loses many of its benefits.

Even managing text-based configuration files can be a hassle. There are many ways for applications to invent their own configuration file formats, but there are a set of base file formats that are popular. Such file formats include XML, YML, JSON, and INI.

Usually, configuration files are not static, because if they were, you could just deploy them with your package system like any piece of binary artifact.

Normally, the application configuration files need to be based on some kind of template file that is later instantiated into a form suitable for the machine where the application is being deployed.

An example might be an application's database connector descriptor. If you are deploying your application to a test environment, you want the connector descriptor to point to a test database server. Vice versa, if you are deploying to a production server, you want your connector to point to a production database server.

As an aside, some organizations try to handle this situation by managing their DNS servers, such that an example database DNS alias `database.yourorg.com` resolves to different servers depending on the environment. The domain `yourorg.com` should be replaced with your organization's details of course, and the database server as well.

Being able to use different DNS resolvers depending on the environment is a useful strategy. It can be difficult for a developer, however, to use the equivalent mechanism on his or her own development machine. Running a private DNS server on a development machine can be difficult, and managing a local host file can also prove cumbersome. In these cases, it might be simpler to make the application have configurable settings for database hosts and other backend systems at the application level.

Many times, it is possible to ignore the details of the actual configuration file format altogether and just rely on the configuration system's template managing system. These usually work by having a special syntax for placeholders that will be replaced by the configuration management system when creating the concrete configuration file for a concrete server, where the application will be deployed. You can use the exact same basic idea for all text-based configuration files, and sometimes even for binary files, even though such hacks should be avoided if at all possible.

The XML format has tools and infrastructure that can be useful in managing configurations, and XML is indeed a popular format for configuration files. For instance, there is a special language, XSLT, to transform XML from one structural form to another. This is very helpful in some cases but used less in practice than one might expect. The simple template macro substitution approach gets you surprisingly far and has the added benefit of being applicable on nearly all text-based configuration formats. XML is also fairly verbose, which also makes it unpopular in some circles. YML can be seen as a reaction to XML's verbosity and can accomplish much of the same things as XML, with less typing.

Another useful feature of some text configuration systems that deserves mention is the idea that a base configuration file can include other configuration files. An example of this is the standard Unix `sudo` tool, which has its base configuration in the `/etc/sudoers` file, but which allows for local customization by including all the files that have been installed in the directory `/etc/sudoers.d`.

This is very convenient, because you can provide a new `sudoer` file without worrying too much about the existing configuration. This allows for a greater degree of modularization, and it is a convenient pattern when the application allows it.

Virtualization stacks

Organizations that have their own internal server farms tend to use virtualization a lot in order to encapsulate the different components of their applications.

There are many different solutions depending on your requirements.

Virtualization solutions provide virtual machines that have virtual hardware, such as network cards and CPUs. Virtualization and container techniques are sometimes confused because they share some similarities.

You can use virtualization techniques to simulate entirely different hardware than the one you have physically. This is commonly referred to as emulation. If you want to emulate mobile phone hardware on your developer machine so that you can test your mobile application, you use virtualization in order to emulate a device. The closer the underlying hardware is to the target platform, the greater the efficiency the emulator can have during emulation. As an example, you can use the QEMU emulator to emulate an Android device. If you emulate an Android x86_64 device on an x86_64-based developer machine, the emulation will be much more efficient than if you emulate an ARM-based Android device on an x86_64-based developer machine.

With server virtualization, you are usually not really interested in the possibility of emulation. You are interested instead in encapsulating your application's server components. For instance, if a server application component starts to run amok and consume unreasonable amounts of CPU time or other resources, you don't want the entire physical machine to stop working altogether.

This can be achieved by creating a virtual machine with, perhaps, two cores on a machine with 64 cores. Only two cores would be affected by the runaway application. The same goes for memory allocation.

Container-based techniques provide similar degrees of encapsulation and control over resource allocation as virtualization techniques do. Containers do not normally provide the emulation features of virtualization, though. This is not an issue since we rarely need emulation for server applications.

The component that abstracts the underlying hardware and arbitrates hardware resources between different competing virtual machines is called a **hypervisor**. The hypervisor can run directly on the hardware, in which case it is called a bare metal hypervisor. Otherwise, it runs inside an operating system with the help of the operating system kernel.

VMware is a proprietary virtualization solution, and exists in desktop and server hypervisor variants. It is well supported and used in many organizations. The server variant changes names sometimes; currently, it's called VMware ESX, which is a bare metal hypervisor.

KVM is a virtualization solution for Linux. It runs inside a Linux host operating system. Since it is an open source solution, it is usually much cheaper than proprietary solutions since there are no licensing costs per instance and is therefore popular with organizations that have massive amounts of virtualization.

Xen is another type of virtualization which, amongst other features, has **paravirtualization**. Paravirtualization is built upon the idea that that if the guest operating system can be made to use a modified kernel, it can execute with greater efficiency. In this way, it sits somewhere between full CPU emulation, where a fully independent kernel version is used, and container-based virtualization, where the host kernel is used.

VirtualBox is an open source virtualization solution from Oracle. It is pretty popular with developers and sometimes used with server installations as well but rarely on a larger scale. Developers who use Microsoft Windows on their developer machines but want to emulate Linux server environments locally often find VirtualBox handy. Likewise, developers who use Linux on their workstations find it useful to emulate Windows machines.

What the different types of virtualization technologies have in common is that they provide APIs in order to allow the automation of virtual machine management. The libvirt API is one such API that can be used with several different underlying hypervisors, such as KVM, QEMU, Xen, and LXC

Executing code on the client

Several of the configuration management systems described here allow you to reuse the node descriptors to execute code on matching nodes. This is sometimes convenient. For example, maybe you want to run a directory listing command on all HTTP servers facing the public Internet, perhaps for debugging purposes.

In the Puppet ecosystem, this command execution system is called Marionette Collective, or MCollective for short.

A note about the exercises

It is pretty easy to try out the various deployment systems using Docker to manage the base operating system, where we will do our experiments. It is a time-saving method that can be used when developing and debugging the deployment code specific to a particular deployment system. This code will then be used for deployments on physical or virtual machines.

We will first try each of the different deployment systems that are usually possible in the local deployment modes. Further down the line, we will see how we can simulate the complete deployment of a system with several containers that together form a virtual cluster.

We will try to use the official Docker images if possible, but sometimes there are none, and sometimes the official image vanishes, as happened with the official Ansible image. Such is life in the fast-moving world of DevOps, for better or for worse.

It should be noted, however, that Docker has some limitations when it comes to emulating a full operating system. Sometimes, a container must run in elevated privilege modes. We will deal with those issues when they arise.

It should also be noted that many people prefer Vagrant for these types of tests. I prefer to use Docker when possible, because it's lightweight, fast, and sufficient most of the time.

Keep in mind that actually deploying systems in production will require more attention to security and other details than we provide here.

The Puppet master and Puppet agents

Puppet is a deployment solution that is very popular in larger organizations and is one of the first systems of its kind.

Puppet consists of a client/server solution, where the client nodes check in regularly with the Puppet server to see if anything needs to be updated in the local configuration.

The Puppet server is called a **Puppet master**, and there is a lot of similar wordplay in the names chosen for the various Puppet components.

Puppet provides a lot of flexibility in handling the complexity of a server farm, and as such, the tool itself is pretty complex.

This is an example scenario of a dialogue between a Puppet client and a Puppet master:

1. The Puppet client decides that it's time to check in with the Puppet master to discover any new configuration changes. This can be due to a timer or manual intervention by an operator at the client. The dialogue between the Puppet client and master is normally encrypted using SSL.

2. The Puppet client presents its credentials so that the Puppet master can know exactly which client is calling. Managing the client credentials is a separate issue.

3. The Puppet master figures out which configuration the client should have by compiling the Puppet catalogue and sending it to the client. This involves a number of mechanisms, and a particular setup doesn't need to utilize all possibilities.

   It is pretty common to have both a role-based and concrete configuration for a Puppet client. Role-based configurations can be inherited.

4. The Puppet master runs the necessary code on the client side such that the configuration matches the one decided on by the Puppet master.

In this sense, a Puppet configuration is declarative. You declare what configuration a machine should have, and Puppet figures out how to get from the current to the desired client state.

There are both pros and cons of the Puppet ecosystem:

- Puppet has a large community, and there are a lot of resources on the Internet for Puppet. There are a lot of different modules, and if you don't have a really strange component to deploy, there already is, with all likelihood, an existing module written for your component that you can modify according to your needs.

- Puppet requires a number of dependencies on the Puppet client machines. Sometimes, this gives rise to problems. The Puppet agent will require a Ruby runtime that sometimes needs to be ahead of the Ruby version available in your distribution's repositories. Enterprise distributions often lag behind in versions.

- Puppet configurations can be complex to write and test.

Ansible

Ansible is a deployment solution that favors simplicity.

The Ansible architecture is agentless; it doesn't need a running daemon on the client side like Puppet does. Instead, the Ansible server logs in to the Ansible node and issues commands over SSH in order to install the required configuration.

While Ansible's agentless architecture does make things simpler, you need a Python interpreter installed on the Ansible nodes. Ansible is somewhat more lenient about the Python version required for its code to run than Puppet is for its Ruby code to run, so this dependence on Python being available is not a great hassle in practice.

Like Puppet and others, Ansible focuses on configuration descriptors that are idempotent. This basically means that the descriptors are declarative and the Ansible system figures out how to bring the server to the desired state. You can rerun the configuration run, and it will be safe, which is not necessarily the case for an imperative system.

Let's try out Ansible with the Docker method we discussed earlier.

We will use the `williamyeh/ansible` image, which has been developed for the purpose, but it should be possible to use any Ansible Docker image or different ones altogether, to which we just add Ansible later.

1. Create a Dockerfile with this statement:
   ```
   FROM williamyeh/ansible:centos7
   ```

2. Build the Docker container with the following command:
   ```
   docker build .
   ```

This will download the image and create an empty Docker container that we can use.

Normally, you would, of course, have a more complex Dockerfile that can add the things we need, but in this case, we are going to use the image interactively, so we will instead mount the directory with Ansible files from the host so that we can change them on the host and rerun them easily.

3. Run the container.

    The following command can be used to run the container. You will need the hash from the previous `build` command:

    ```
    docker run -v `pwd`/ansible:/ansible  -it <hash> bash
    ```

    Now we have a prompt, and we have Ansible available. The `-v` trick is to make parts of the host filesystem visible to the Docker guest container. The files will be visible in the `/ansible` directory in the container.

The `playbook.yml` file is as follows:

```
---
- hosts: localhost
  vars:
    http_port: 80
    max_clients: 200
  remote_user: root
  tasks:
  - name: ensure apache is at the latest version
    yum: name=httpd state=latest
```

This playbook doesn't do very much, but it demonstrates some concepts of Ansible playbooks.

Now, we can try to run our Ansible playbook:

```
cd /ansible

ansible-playbook -i inventory playbook.yml     --connection=local --sudo
```

The output will look like this:

```
PLAY [localhost] ************************************************************
******

GATHERING FACTS ************************************************************
******
ok: [localhost]
```

```
TASK: [ensure apache is at the latest version] *************************
******

ok: [localhost]


PLAY RECAP ************************************************************
******

localhost                  : ok=2    changed=0    unreachable=0
failed=0
```

Tasks are run to ensure the state we want. In this case, we want to install Apache's httpd using yum, and we want httpd to be the latest version.

To proceed further with our exploration, we might like to do more things, such as starting services automatically. However, here we run into a limitation with the approach of using Docker to emulate physical or virtual hosts. Docker is a container technology, after all, and not a full-blown virtualization system. In Docker's normal use case scenarios, this doesn't matter, but in our case, we need make some workarounds in order to proceed. The main problem is that the systemd init system requires special care to run in a container. Developers at Red Hat have worked out methods of doing this. The following is a slightly modified version of a Docker image by Vaclav Pavlin, who works with Red Hat:

```
FROM fedora
RUN yum -y update; yum clean all
RUN yum install  ansible sudo
RUN systemctl mask systemd-remount-fs.service dev-hugepages.mount sys-
fs-fuse-connections.mount systemd-logind.service getty.target console-
getty.service
RUN cp /usr/lib/systemd/system/dbus.service /etc/systemd/system/; sed
-i 's/OOMScoreAdjust=-900//' /etc/systemd/system/dbus.service

VOLUME ["/sys/fs/cgroup", "/run", "/tmp"]
ENV container=docker

CMD ["/usr/sbin/init"]
```

The environment variable container is used to tell the systemd init system that it runs inside a container and to behave accordingly.

We need some more arguments for docker run in order to enable systemd to work in the container:

```
docker run -it --rm -v /sys/fs/cgroup:/sys/fs/cgroup:ro  -v `pwd`/
ansible:/ansible <hash>
```

The container boots with `systemd`, and now we need to connect to the running container from a different shell:

```
docker exec -it <hash> bash
```

Phew! That was quite a lot of work just to get the container more lifelike! On the other hand, working with virtual machines, such as VirtualBox, is even more cumbersome in my opinion. The reader might, of course, decide differently.

Now, we can run a slightly more advanced Ansible playbook inside the container, as follows:

```
---
- hosts: localhost
  vars:
    http_port: 80
    max_clients: 200
  remote_user: root
  tasks:
  - name: ensure apache is at the latest version
    yum: name=httpd state=latest
  - name: write the apache config file
    template: src=/srv/httpd.j2 dest=/etc/httpd.conf
    notify:
    - restart apache
  - name: ensure apache is running (and enable it at boot)
    service: name=httpd state=started enabled=yes
  handlers:
    - name: restart apache
      service: name=httpd state=restarted
```

This example builds on the previous one, and shows you how to:

- Install a package
- Write a template file
- Handle the running state of a service

The format is in a pretty simple YML syntax.

PalletOps

PalletOps is an advanced deployment system, which combines the declarative power of Lisp with a very lightweight server configuration.

PalletOps takes Ansible's agentless idea one step further. Rather than needing a Ruby or Python interpreter installed on the node that is to be configured, you only need `ssh` and a `bash` installation. These are pretty simple requirements.

PalletOps compiles its Lisp-defined DSL to Bash code that is executed on the slave node. These are such simple requirements that you can use it on very small and simple servers—even phones!

On the other hand, while there are a number of support modules for Pallet called **crates**, there are fewer of them than there are for Puppet or Ansible.

Deploying with Chef

Chef is a Ruby-based deployment system from Opscode.

It is pretty easy to try out Chef; for fun, we can do it in a Docker container so we don't pollute our host environment with our experiments:

```
docker run -it ubuntu
```

We need the `curl` command to proceed with downloading the chef installer:

```
apt-get -y install curl
curl -L https://www.opscode.com/chef/install.sh | bash
```

The Chef installer is built with a tool from the Chef team called **omnibus**. Our aim here is to try out a Chef tool called `chef-solo`. Verify that the tool is installed:

```
chef-solo -v
```

This will give output as:

```
Chef: 12.5.1
```

The point of `chef-solo` is to be able to run configuration scripts without the full infrastructure of the configuration system, such as the client/server setup. This type of testing environment is often useful when working with configuration systems, since it can be hard to get all the bits and pieces in working order while developing the configuration that you are going to deploy.

Chef prefers a file structure for its files, and a pre-rolled structure can be retrieved from GitHub. You can download and extract it with the following commands:

```
curl -L  http://github.com/opscode/chef-repo/tarball/master -o master.tgz
tar -zxf master.tgz
mv chef-chef-repo* chef-repo
rm master.tgz
```

You will now have a suitable file structure prepared for Chef cookbooks, which looks like the following:

```
./cookbooks
./cookbooks/README.md
./data_bags
./data_bags/README.md
./environments
./environments/README.md
./README.md
./LICENSE
./roles
./roles/README.md
./chefignore
```

You will need to perform a further step to make everything work properly, telling `chef` where to find its cookbooks as:

```
mkdir .chef
echo "cookbook_path [ '/root/chef-repo/cookbooks' ]" > .chef/knife.rb
```

Now we can use the `knife` tool to create a template for a configuration, as follows:

```
knife cookbook create phpapp
```

Deploying with SaltStack

SaltStack is a Python-based deployment solution.

There is a convenient dockerized test environment for Salt, by Jackson Cage. You can start it with the following:

```
docker run -i -t --name=saltdocker_master_1 -h master -p 4505 -p 4506 \
   -p 8080 -p 8081 -e SALT_NAME=master -e SALT_USE=master \
   -v `pwd`/srv/salt:/srv/salt:rw jacksoncage/salt
```

This will create a single container with both a Salt master and a Salt minion.

We can create a shell inside the container for our further explorations:

```
docker exec -i -t saltdocker_master_1 bash
```

We need a configuration to apply to our server. Salt calls configurations "states", or Salt states.

In our case, we want to install an Apache server with this simple Salt state:

```
top.sls:
base:
  '*':
    - webserver


webserver.sls:
apache2:                # ID declaration
  pkg:                  # state declaration
    - installed         # function declaration
```

Salt uses .yml files for its configuration files, similar to what Ansible does.

The file top.sls declares that all matching nodes should be of the type webserver. The webserver state declares that an apache2 package should be installed, and that's basically it. Please note that this will be distribution dependent. The Salt Docker test image we are using is based on Ubuntu, where the Apache web server package is called apache2. On Fedora for instance, the Apache web server package is instead simply called httpd.

Run the command once to see Salt in action, by making Salt read the Salt state and apply it locally:

```
salt-call --local state.highstate -l debug
```

The first run will be very verbose, especially since we enabled the debug flag!

Now, let's run the command again:

```
salt-call --local state.highstate -l debug
```

This will also be pretty verbose, and the output will end with this:

```
local:
----------
          ID: apache2
    Function: pkg.installed
      Result: True
     Comment: Package apache2 is already installed.
     Started: 22:55:36.937634
    Duration: 2267.167 ms
```

```
    Changes:

Summary
------------
Succeeded: 1
Failed:    0
------------
Total states run:      1
```

Now, you can quit the container and restart it. This will clean the container from the Apache instance installed during the previous run.

This time, we will apply the same state but use the message queue method rather than applying the state locally:

```
salt-call state.highstate
```

This is the same command as used previously, except we omitted the -local flag. You could also try running the command again and verify that the state remains the same.

Salt versus Ansible versus Puppet versus PalletOps execution models

While the configuration systems we explore in this chapter share a fair number of similarities, they differ a lot in the way code is executed on the client nodes:

- With Puppet, a Puppet agent registers with the Puppet master and opens a communication channel to retrieve commands. This process is repeated periodically, normally every thirty minutes.

> Thirty minutes isn't fast. You can, of course, configure a lower value for the time interval required for the next run. At any rate, Puppet essentially uses a pull model. Clients must check in to know whether changes are available.

- Ansible pushes changes over SSH when desired. This is a push model.
- Salt uses a push model, but with a different implementation. It employs a ZeroMQ messaging server that the clients connect to and listen for notifications about changes. This works a bit like Puppet, but faster.

Which method is best is an area of contention between developer communities. Proponents of the message queue architecture believe that it is faster and that speed matters. Proponents of the plain SSH method claim that it is fast enough and that simplicity matters. I lean toward the latter stance. Things tend to break, and the likelihood of breakage increases with complexity.

Vagrant

Vagrant is a configuration system for virtual machines. It is geared towards creating virtual machines for developers, but it can be used for other purposes as well.

Vagrant supports several virtualization providers, and VirtualBox is a popular provider for developers.

First, some preparation. Install `vagrant` according to the instructions for your distribution. For Fedora, the command is this:

```
yum install 'vagrant*'
```

This will install a number of packages. However, as we are installing this on Fedora, we will experience some problems. The Fedora Vagrant packages use `libvirt` as a virtual machine provider rather than VirtualBox. That is useful in many cases, but in this case, we would like to use VirtualBox as a provider, which requires some extra steps on Fedora. If you use some other distribution, the case might be different.

First, add the VirtualBox repository to your Fedora installation. Then we can install VirtualBox with the `dnf` command, as follows:

```
dnf install VirtualBox
```

VirtualBox is not quite ready to be used yet, though. It needs special kernel modules to work, since it needs to arbitrate access to low-level resources. The VirtualBox kernel driver is not distributed with the Linux kernel. Managing Linux kernel drivers outside of the Linux source tree has always been somewhat inconvenient compared to the ease of using kernel drivers that are always installed by default. The VirtualBox kernel driver can be installed as a source module that needs to be compiled. This process can be automated to a degree with the `dkms` command, which will recompile the driver as needed when there is a new kernel installed. The other method, which is easier and less error-prone, is to use a kernel module compiled for your kernel by your distribution. If your distribution provides a kernel module, it should be loaded automatically. Otherwise, you could try `modprobe vboxdrv`. For some distributions, you can compile the driver by calling an `init.d` script as follows:

```
sudo /etc/init.d/vboxdrv setup
```

Now that the Vagrant dependencies are installed, we can bring up a Vagrant virtual machine.

The following command will create a Vagrant configuration file from a template. We will be able to change this file later. The base image will be hashicorp/precise32, which in turn is based on Ubuntu.

```
vagrant init hashicorp/precise32
```

Now, we can start the machine:

```
vagrant up
```

If all went well, we should have a vagrant virtual machine instance running now, but since it is headless, we won't see anything.

Vagrant shares some similarities with Docker. Docker uses base images that can be extended. Vagrant also allows this. In the Vagrant vocabulary, a base image is called a **box**.

To connect to the headless vagrant instance we started previously, we can use this command:

```
vagrant ssh
```

Now we have an ssh session, where we can work with the virtual machine. For this to work, Vagrant has taken care of a couple of tasks, such as setting up keys for the SSH communication channel for us.

Vagrant also provides a configuration system so that Vagrant machine descriptors can be used to recreate a virtual machine that is completely configured from source code.

Here is the Vagrantfile we got from the earlier stage. Comments are removed for brevity.

```
Vagrant.configure(2) do |config|
  config.vm.box = "hashicorp/precise32"
end
```

Add a line to the Vagrantfile that will call the bash script that we will provide:

```
Vagrant.configure("2") do |config|
  config.vm.box = "hashicorp/precise32"
  config.vm.provision :shell, path: "bootstrap.sh"
end
```

The `bootstrap.sh` script will look like this:

```
#!/usr/bin/env bash
apt-get update
apt-get install -y apache2
```

This will install an Apache web server in the Vagrant-managed virtual machine.

Now we know enough about Vagrant to be able to reason about it from a DevOps perspective:

- Vagrant is a convenient way of managing configurations primarily for virtual machines based on VirtualBox. It's great for testing.
- The configuration method doesn't really scale up to clusters, and it's not the intended use case, either.
- On the other hand, several configuration systems such as Ansible support Vagrant, so Vagrant can be very useful while testing our configuration code.

Deploying with Docker

A recent alternative for deployment is Docker, which has several very interesting traits. We have already used Docker several times in this book.

You can make use of Docker's features for test automation purposes even if you use, for instance, Puppet or Ansible to deploy your products.

Docker's model of creating reusable containers that can be used on development machines, testing environments, and production environments is very appealing.

At the time of writing, Docker is beginning to have an impact on larger enterprises, but solutions such as Puppet are dominant.

While it is well known how to build large Puppet or Ansible server farms, it's not yet equally well known how to build large Docker-based server clusters.

There are several emerging solutions, such as these:

- **Docker Swarm:** Docker Swarm is compatible with Docker Compose, which is appealing. Docker Swarm is maintained by the Docker community.
- **Kubernetes**: Kubernetes is modeled after Google's Borg cluster software, which is appealing since it's a well-tested model used in-house in Google's vast data centers. Kubernetes is not the same as Borg though, which must be kept in mind. It's not clear whether Kubernetes offers scaling the same way Borg does.

Comparison tables

Everyone likes coming up with new words for old concepts. While the different concepts in various products don't always match, it's tempting to make a dictionary that maps the configuration systems' different terminology with each other.

Here is such a terminology comparison chart:

System	Puppet	Ansible	Pallet	Salt
Client	Agent	Node	Node	Minion
Server	Master	Server	Server	Master
Configuration	Catalog	Playbook	Crate	Salt State

Also, here is a technology comparison chart:

System	Puppet	Ansible	Pallet	Chef	Salt
Agentless	No	Yes	Yes	Yes	Both
Client dependencies	Ruby	Python, sshd, bash	sshd, bash	Ruby, sshd, bash	Python
Language	Ruby	Python	Clojure	Ruby	Python

Cloud solutions

First, we must take a step back and have a look at the landscape. We can either use a cloud provider, such as AWS or Azure, or we can use our own internal cloud solution, such as VMware or OpenStack. There are valid arguments for both external and internal cloud providers or even both, depending on your organization.

Some types of organizations, such as government agencies, must store all data regarding citizens within their own walls. Such organizations can't use external cloud providers and services and must instead build their own internal cloud equivalents.

Smaller private organizations might benefit from using an external cloud provider but can't perhaps afford having all their resources with such a provider. They might opt to have in-house servers for normal loads and scale out to an external cloud provider during peak loads.

Many of the configuration systems we have described here support the management of cloud nodes as well as local nodes. PalletOps supports AWS and Puppet supports Azure, for instance. Ansible supports a host of different cloud services.

AWS

Amazon Web Services allows us to deploy virtual machine images on Amazon's clusters. You can also deploy Docker images. Follow these steps to set up AWS:

1. Sign up for an account with AWS. Registration is free of charge, but a credit card number is required even for the free of charge tier

2. Some identity verification will need to happen, which can be done via an automated challenge-response phone call.

3. When the user verification process is complete, you will be able to log in to AWS and use the web console.

> In my opinion, the AWS web console does not represent the epitome of web interface usability, but it gets the job done. There are a host of options, and in our case, we are interested in the virtual machine and Docker container options.

4. Go to **EC2 network and security**. Here you can create management keys that will be required later.

   As a first example, let's create the default container example provided by AWS, console-sample-app-static. To log in to the generated server, you need first to create an SSH key pair and upload your public key to AWS. Click through all the steps and you will get a small sample cluster. The final resource creation step can be slow, so it's the perfect opportunity to grab a cup of coffee!

5. Now, we can view the details of the cluster and choose the web server container. You can see the IP address. Try opening it in a web browser.

Now that we have a working account on AWS, we can manage it with the configuration management system of our choosing.

Azure

Azure is a cloud platform from Microsoft. It can host both Linux and Microsoft virtual machines. While AWS is the service people often default to, at least in the Linux space, it never hurts to explore the options. Azure is one such option that is gaining market share at the moment.

Creating a virtual machine on Azure for evaluation purposes is comparable to creating a virtual machine on AWS. The process is fairly smooth.

Summary

In this chapter, we explored some of the many options available to us when deploying the code we built. There are a lot many options, and that is for a reason. Deployment is a difficult subject, and you will likely spend a lot of time figuring out which option suits you best.

In the next chapter, we will explore the topic of monitoring our running code.

8
Monitoring the Code

In the previous chapter, we explored methods of deploying our code.

Now that the code has been safely deployed to your servers with the deployment solution of your choice, you need to watch over it to make sure it's running properly. You can spend a lot of time preparing for the many modes of failure that you may envision during development. In the end, your software will probably break for other reasons altogether than those you prepared for. If your system breaks, it can be very expensive for your organization, either in lost revenue or in terms of lost credibility, which, in the end, might amount to the same thing. You need to know as quickly as possible what has gone wrong in order to deal with the situation.

Given the potential negative impact of service downtime, there are many alternative solutions that approach the problem domain of watching over your deployed code from different angles and viewpoints.

In this chapter, we will have a look at several of the options that are available to us.

Nagios

In this section, we will explore the Nagios monitoring solution for overall server health.

Nagios has been around since 1999 and has a large community that provides plugins and extensions for various needs. There are extensive resources available for Nagios on the web, and commercial support if your organization requires it.

Since it has been around so long and many organizations use it, Nagios is the standard in network monitoring against which other solutions compare themselves. As such, it is the natural starting point for our journey through the monitoring landscape.

The name Nagios is a recursive acronym, which is a tradition in hacker circles. It stands for "Nagios Ain't Gonna Insist On Sainthood". Originally, the product was called NetSaint, but the name was rejected in favor of the Nagios acronym during a trademark dispute. The word *agios* also means *angel* in Greek, so it is a pretty clever acronym overall.

Here are some screenshots from a small demo Nagios installation. Nagios provides many views, and here we see two of them:

- **Service Overview For All Host Groups**:

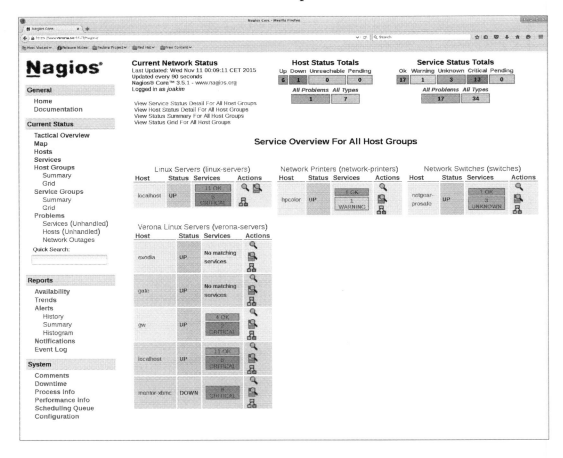

- **Service Status Details For All Hosts**:

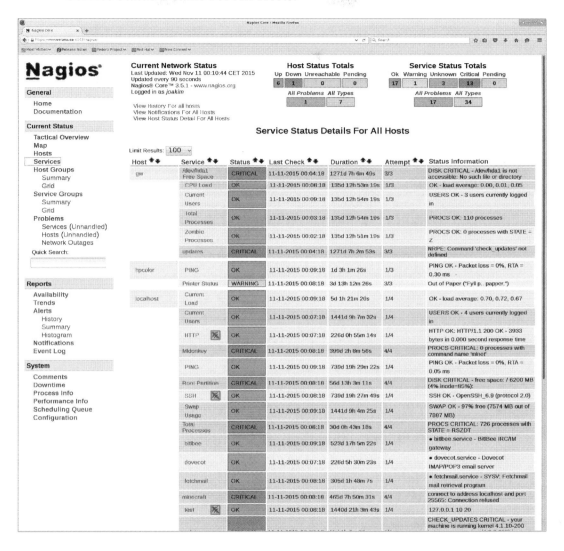

The views indicate some example problems, as follows:

- ° A host is unreachable
- ° A disk in one of the hosts is getting full

A host has pending updates available. Let's now examine the basics of Nagios in particular and monitoring in general with a simple scenario:

- We have a Nagios host that monitors the well-being of a number of other physical and virtual hosts.

- One of the hosts being monitored, a web server, suddenly vanishes from the network altogether. Nagios knows this, since it is set up to ping the web server every five minutes and take action in the event that the server does not respond to the pings in a timely fashion.

- Nagios determines what to do when this server is down, which in this case is to send an e-mail to everyone in a predetermined group (in this case, the administrators of the organization).

- Joakim, who happens to be around the Matangle office, is the first to respond to the e-mail, and goes down to the quite unprofessional server room in the cellar. The web server has stopped working because its power supply unit is full of dust, which accumulated there while renovations were being done in a nearby room — sawing plaster generates a lot of dust. Joakim curses and vows that he would move the servers to better hosting, if he only had the resources.

You likely take better care of your servers than Joakim did in this scenario, but the point is that unforeseen things happen, and Nagios was helpful in resolving the situation. Also, while employing a proper data center for your servers might prevent things such as dust in your equipment and people tripping over network cables, there are still any number of weird and unforeseen modes of failure present in the unforgiving world of complex server deployments.

Nagios can monitor services as well as hosts and can utilize different methods to do so. The simplest methods work on the Nagios server and query a service on a remote host.

Nagios differentiates between two basic classes of checks:

- **Active checks**: These are initiated by Nagios. Nagios can execute code in plugins regularly. The outcome of the code execution determines whether the check fails or not. Active checks are the most common and are useful and easy to set up with many types of services, such as HTTP, SSH, and databases.

- **Passive checks**: These originate from a system other than Nagios, and the system notifies Nagios rather than Nagios polling it. These are useful in special situations, for instance, if the service being monitored is behind a firewall or if the service is asynchronous and it would be inefficient to monitor it with polling.

Configuring Nagios is relatively straightforward if you are used to file-based configuration, but there is a lot of configuring to do in order to get basic functionality.

We are going to explore Nagios with the Docker Hub image `cpuguy83/nagios`. The image uses Nagios version 3.5, which is the same version available in the Fedora repositories at the time of writing. There are later versions of Nagios available, but many still seem to prefer the version 3 series. The `cpuguy83` image takes the approach of downloading Nagios tarballs from SourceForge and installing them inside the image. If you prefer, you can use this same approach to install the Nagios version of your choosing. There is an alternative Docker file in the book sources, and in case you use it, you will need to build the image locally.

This statement starts a Nagios server container:

```
docker run -e    NAGIOSADMIN_USER=nagiosadmin -e NAGIOSAMDIN_PASS=nagios
-p 80:30000 cpuguy83/nagios
```

Verify that the Nagios web interface is available on port 30000; enter the username and password defined above to log in.

The out-of-the-box configuration of the Nagios user interface allows you to browse, amongst other things, hosts and services, but the only host defined at the outset is the localhost, which in this case is the container running Nagios itself. We will now configure another host to monitor, in the form of a separate Docker container. This will allow us to bring the monitored container down by force and verify that the Nagios container notices the outage.

This command will start a second container running `nginx` in the default configuration:

```
docker run -p 30001:80 nginx
```

Verify that the container is running by going to `port 30001`. You will see a simple message, `Welcome to nginx!`. This is more or less all that this container does out of the box, which is good enough for our test. You can, of course, use a physical host instead if you prefer.

To run the containers together, we can either link them on the command line or use a Docker compose file. Here is a Docker compose file for this scenario, which is also available in the book sources:

```
nagios:
 image: mt-nagios
 build:
   - mt-nagios
```

```
ports:
  -  80:30000
environment:
   - NAGIOSADMIN_USER=nagiosadmin
   - NAGIOSAMDIN_PASS=nagios
volumes:
  ./nagios:/etc/nagios
nginx:
 image: nginx
```

The Nagios configuration is mounted in the `./nagios` directory as a Docker volume.

The configuration required for Nagios to monitor the `nginx` container is available in the sources and is also included here:

```
define host {
    name             regular-host
    use              linux-server
    register         0
    max_check_attempts   5
}

define host{
    use              regular-host
    host_name        client1
    address          192.168.200.15
    contact_groups   admins
    notes            test client1
}
hostgroups.cfg
define hostgroup {
    hostgroup_name   test-group
    alias            Test Servers
    members          client1
}

services.cfg
#+BEGIN_SRC sh
define service {
    use                   generic-service
    hostgroup_name        test-group
    service_description   PING
    check_command         check_ping!200.0,20%!600.0,60%
}
```

Let's see what happens when we bring the `nginx` container down.

Find out the hash of the `nginx` container with `docker ps`. Then kill it with `docker kill`. Verify that the container is really gone with `docker ps` again.

Now, wait a while and reload the Nagios web user interface. You should see that Nagios has alerted you of the situation.

This will look similar to the earlier screenshots that showed faulty services.

Now, you would like to have an e-mail when NGINX goes down. It is, however, not straightforward to make an example that works in a foolproof way, simply since e-mail is more complicated these days due to spam. You need to know your mail server details, such as the SMTP server details. Here is a skeleton you need to fill out with your particular details:

You can create a file `contacts.cfg` for handling e-mail, with the following contents:

```
define contact{
    contact_name              matangle-admin
    use                       generic-contact
    alias                     Nagios Admin
    email                     pd-admin@matangle.com
}

define contactgroup{
    contactgroup_name     admins
    alias                 Nagios Administrators
    members               matange-admin
}
```

 If you don't change this configuration, the mail will wind up at `pd-admin@matangle.com`, which will be ignored.

Munin

Munin is used to graph server statistics such as memory usage, which is useful in order to understand overall server health. Since Munin graphs statistics over time, you can see resource allocation trends, which can help you find problems before they get serious. There are several other applications like Munin that create graphs; however, like Nagios, Munin is a good starting point.

It is designed to be easy to use and set up. The out-of-the-box experience gives you many graphs with little work.

In the legends of the Norse, Hugin and Munin were two pitch-black ravens. They tirelessly flew around the world of Midgard and collected information. After their journeys far and wide, they returned to the god king Odin to sit on his shoulders and tell him all about their experiences. The name Hugin derives from the word for thought and Munin from the word for memory.

While Nagios focuses on the high-level traits of the health of a service (whether the service or host is alive or not in binary terms), Munin keeps track of statistics that it periodically samples, and draws graphs of them.

Munin can sample a lot of different types of statistics, from CPU and memory load to the number of active users in your children's Minecraft server. It is also easy to make plugins that get you the statistics you want from your own services.

An image can say a lot and convey lots of information at a glance, so graphing the memory and processor load of your servers can give you an early warning if something is about to go wrong.

Here is an example screenshot of Munin, displaying metrics for a firewall installation at the Matangle headquarters:

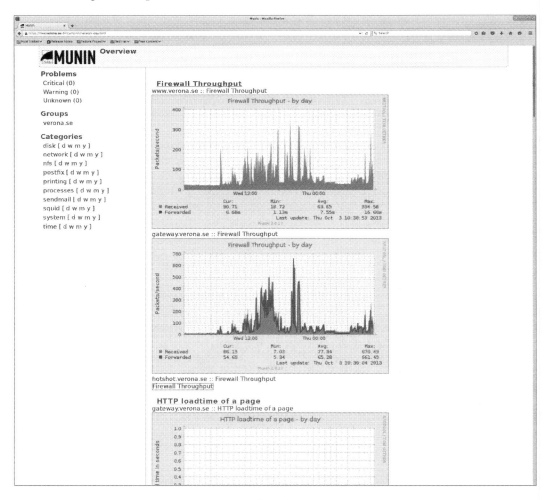

And here are some metrics for the organization's `smtpd`, a Postfix installation:

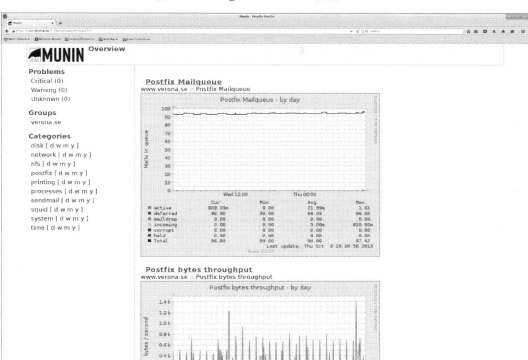

Like any of the monitoring systems we are exploring in this chapter, Munin also has a network-oriented architecture, as explained here. It is similar in design to Nagios. The main components of Munin are as follows:

- There is a central server, the Munin master, which is responsible for gathering data from the Munin nodes. The Munin data is stored in a database system called **RRD**, which is an acronym for **Round-robin Database**. The RRD also does the graphing of the gathered data.

- The Munin node is a component that is installed on the servers that will be monitored. The Munin master connects to all the Munin nodes and runs plugins which return data to the master.

To try it out, we will again use a Docker container running the service we are exploring, Munin:

```
docker run -p 30005:80 lrivallain/munin:latest
```

Munin will take a while to run the first time, so wait a while before checking the web interface. If you don't like to wait, you can run the munin-update command by hand in the container, as shown here. It polls all the Munin nodes for statistics explicitly.

```
docker run exec -it <hash> bash
su - munin --shell=/bin/bash
/usr/share/munin/munin-update
```

Now you should be able to see the graphs created during the first update. If you let the stack run for a while, you can see how the graphs develop.

It is not very hard to write a Munin plugin that monitors a statistic specific to your application stack. You can make a shell script that Munin calls in order to get the statistics you want to track.

Munin itself is written in Perl, but you can write Munin plugins in most languages as long as you conform to the very simple interface.

The program should return some metadata when called with a config argument. This is so that Munin can put proper labels on the graphs.

Here is an example graph configuration:

```
graph_title Load average
graph_vlabel load
load.label load
```

To emit data you simply print it to stdout.

```
printf "load.value "
cut -d' ' -f2  /proc/loadavg
```

Here is an example script that will graph the machine's load average:

```
#!/bin/sh

case $1 in
   config)
        cat <<'EOM'
graph_title Load average
graph_vlabel load
load.label load
EOM
        exit 0;;
esac

printf "load.value "
cut -d' ' -f2  /proc/loadavg
```

This system is pretty simple and reliable, and you can probably easily implement it for your application. All you need to do is be able to print your statistics to stdout.

Ganglia

Ganglia is a graphing and monitoring solution for large clusters. It can aggregate information in convenient overview displays.

The word "ganglia" is the plural form of ganglion, which is a nerve cell cluster in anatomy. The analogy implies that Ganglia can be the sensory nerve cell network in your cluster.

Like Munin, Ganglia also uses RRDs for database storage and graphing, so the graphs will look similar to the previous Munin graphs. Code reuse is a good thing!

Ganglia has an interesting online demonstration at http://ganglia.wikimedia. org/latest/.

Wikimedia serves media content for Wikipedia, which is pretty busy. The demonstration thus gives us a good overview of Ganglia's capabilities, which would be hard to get in any easy way in your own network.

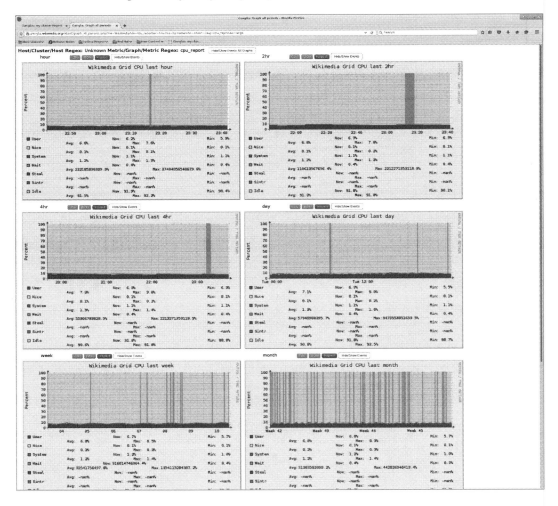

The first page shows an overview of the available data in graph format. You can drill down in the graphs to get other perspectives.

If you drill down one of the application cluster graphs for CPU load, for example, you get a detailed view of the individual servers in the cluster. You can click on a server node to drill down further.

If you have the kind of cluster scale that Wikimedia has, you can clearly see the attraction of Ganglia overviews and drill-down views. You have both a view from orbit and the details easily accessible together.

Ganglia consists of the following components:

- **Gmond**: This is an acronym for **Ganglia monitoring daemon**. Gmond is a service that collects information about a node. Gmond will need to be installed on each server that you want Ganglia to monitor.

- **Gmetad**: This stands for **Ganglia meta daemon**. Gmetad is a daemon which runs on the master node, collecting the information that all the Gmond nodes gather. Gmetad daemons can also work together to spread the load across the network. If you have a large enough cluster, the topology does indeed start to look like a nerve cell network!

- **RRD**: A round-robin database, the same tool Munin uses on the master node to store data and visualizations for Ganglia in time series that are suitable for graphing.

- **A PHP-based web frontend:** This displays the data that the master node has collected and RRD has graphed for us.

Compared to Munin, Ganglia has an extra layer, the meta daemon. This extra layer allows Ganglia to scale by distributing the network load between nodes.

Ganglia has a grid concept, where you group clusters with a similar purpose together. You can, for example, put all your database servers together in a grid. The database servers don't need to have any other relationship; they can serve different applications. The grid concept allows you to view the performance metrics of all your database servers together.

You can define grids in any manner you like: it can be convenient to view servers by location, by application, or any other logical grouping you need.

You can try Ganglia out locally as well, again, using a Docker image.

The `wookietreiber/ganglia` Docker image from Docker Hub offers some inbuilt help:

```
docker run wookietreiber/ganglia --help

Usage: docker run wookietreiber/ganglia [opts]

Run a ganglia-web container.

  -? | -h | -help | --help          print this help
  --with-gmond                      also run gmond inside the
container
  --without-gmond                   do not run gmond inside the
container
  --timezone arg                    set timezone within the
container,
                                    must be path below /usr/share/
zoneinfo,
                                    e.g. Europe/Berlin
```

In our case, we will run the image with the following command-line arguments:

```
docker run -p 30010:80 wookietreiber/ganglia
```

This image runs Gmond as well as Gmetad. This means that it will monitor itself out of the box. We will add a separate container running Gmetad in a moment.

Now that the Ganglia container is running, you can check out the web interface served by the container:

```
http://localhost:30010/ganglia/
```

The browser should show a view similar to the following screenshot:

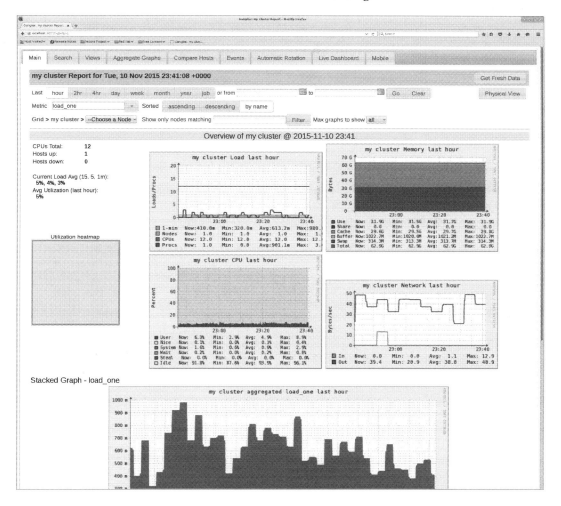

Ganglia Gmond nodes communicate between themselves on a multicast IP channel. This offers redundancy and ease of configuration in large clusters, and the multicast configuration is default. You can also configure Ganglia in unicast mode.

Since we will only run with two communicating containers, we will not actually benefit from the multicast configuration in this case.

Again, we will use Docker Compose to start the containers together so that the separate Gmond and Gmetad instances can communicate. We can start three containers that all run `gmond`. The Gmetad daemon will in the default configuration discover them and list them together under `My Cluster`:

```
gmetad:
  image: wookietreiber/ganglia
  ports:
    - "30010:80"
gmond:
  image: wookietreiber/ganglia
gmond2:
  image: wookietreiber/ganglia
```

When you access `http://localhost:30010/ganglia/`, you should find the new `gmond` instance being monitored.

Graphite

While Munin is nice because it is robust and fairly easy to start using, the graphs it provides are only updated once in a while, normally every fifth minute. There is therefore a niche for a tool that does graphing that is closer to real time. Graphite is such a tool.

The Graphite stack consists of the following three major parts. It is similar to both Ganglia and Munin but uses its own component implementations.

- The Graphite Web component, which is a web application that renders a user interface consisting of graphs and dashboards organized within a tree-like browser widget

- The Carbon metric processing daemon, which gathers the metrics

- The Whisper time series database library

As such, the Graphite stack is similar in utility to both Munin and Ganglia. Unlike Munin and Ganglia though, it uses its own time series library, Whisper, rather than an RRD.

There are several prepackaged Docker images for trying out Graphite. We can use the `sitespeedio/graphite` image from the Docker Hub, as follows:

```
docker run -it \ -p 30020:80 \ -p 2003:2003 \ sitespeedio/graphite
```

This starts a Docker container running Graphite with HTTP Basic authentication.

You can now view the user interface of Graphite. Enter "guest" for both the username and password. You can change the username and password by providing a .htpasswd file for the image.

If you don't change the port in the Docker statement above, this URL should work:

```
http://localhost:30020/
```

The browser window should display a view similar to the following screenshot:

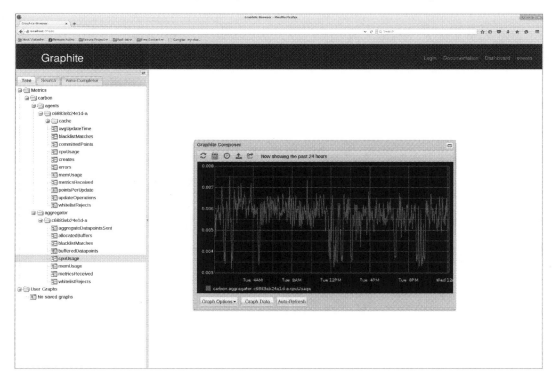

Graphite has a customizable user interface, where you can organize the graphs in which you are interested together in dashboards. There is also a completion widget that lets you find named graphs by typing the first few characters of a graph name.

Log handling

Log handling is a very important concept, and we will explore some of the many options, such as the **ELK** (**Elasticsearch**, **Logstash** and **Kibana**) stack.

Traditionally, logging just consisted of using simple print statements in code to trace events in the code. This is sometimes called **printf-style debugging**, because you use traces to see how your code behaves rather than using a regular debugger.

Here is a simple example in C syntax. The idea is that we want to know when we enter the function *fn(x)* and what value the argument *x* has:

```
void fn(char *x){
  printf("DEBUG entering fn, x is %s\n", x);
  ...
}
```

From the debug traces in the console, you can determine whether the program being developed is behaving as expected.

You would, of course, also like to see whether something serious is wrong with your program and report that with a higher priority:

```
printf("ERROR x cant be an empty string\n");
```

There are several problems with this style of debugging. They are useful when you want to know how the program behaves, but they are not so useful when you have finished developing and want to deploy your code.

Today, there are a great number of frameworks that support logging in many different ways, based on the time-proven pattern above.

The logging frameworks add value to printf-style logging primarily by defining standards and offering improved functionality such as these:

- Different log priorities, such as Debug, Warning, Trace, and Error.
- Filtering log messages of different priorities. You might not always be interested in debug traces, but you are probably always interested in error messages.

- Logging to different destinations, such as files, databases, or network daemons. This includes the ELK stack that we will visit later.

- The rotating and archiving of log files. Old log files can be archived.

Every now and then, a new logging framework pops up, so the logging problem domain seems far from exhausted even to this day. This tendency is understandable, since properly done logs can help you determine the exact cause of the failure of a network service that is no longer running or, of course, any complicated service that you are not constantly supervising. Logging is also hard to do right, since excessive logging can kill the performance of your service, and too little doesn't help you determine the cause of failures. Therefore, logging systems go to great lengths to strike a balance between the various traits of logging.

Client-side logging libraries

Log4j is a popular logging framework for Java. There are several ports for other languages, such as:

- **Log4c** for the C language
- **Log4js** for the JavaScript language
- **Apache log4net**, a port to the Microsoft .NET framework

Several other ports exist, with many different logging frameworks that share many of their concepts.

Since there are many logging frameworks for the Java platform alone, there are also some wrapper logging frameworks, such as **Apache Commons Logging** or **Simple Logging Facade for Java (SLF4J)**. These are intended to allow you to use a single interface and swap out the underlying logging framework implementation if needed.

Logback is meant to be the successor of log4j and is compatible with the ELK stack.

Log4j is the first of the Java logging frameworks, and essentially gives you the equivalent of the previous `printf` statements but with many more bells and whistles.

Log4j works with three primary constructs:

- Loggers
- Appenders
- Layouts

The logger is the class you use to access logging methods. There's a logging method to call for each log severity. Loggers are also hierarchical.

These concepts are easiest to explain with some example code:

```
Logger  logger = Logger.getLogger("se.matangle");
```

This gets us a logger specific to our organization. In this way, we can make out our own logger messages from messages that originate with other organizations' code that we might be using. This becomes very useful in a Java enterprise environment, where you might have dozens of libraries that all use log4j for their logging and you want to be able to configure different log levels for each library.

We can use several loggers at the same time for greater granularity of our logs. Different software components can have different loggers.

Here is an example from a video recording application:

```
Logger  videologger = Logger.getLogger("se.matangle.video");
logger.warn("disk is dangerously low")
```

We can use several different log levels, adding greater specificity to our logs:

```
videologger.error("video encoding source running out prematurely")
```

The place where the log message winds up in the end is called an **appender** in log4j terminology. There are a number of appenders available, such as the console, files, network destinations, and logger daemons.

Layouts control how our log messages will be formatted. They allow for escape sequences with printf-like formatting.

For example, the class `PatternLayout` configured to use the conversion pattern `%r [%t] %-5p %c - %m%n` will create the following example output:

176 [main] INFO se.matangle - User found

Here's what the fields in the pattern stand for:

- The first field is the number of milliseconds elapsed since the start of the program
- The second field is the thread making the log request
- The third field is the level of the log statement
- The fourth field is the name of the logger associated with the log request
- The text after the - is the message of the statement

Log4j endeavors to make the configuration of the logging external to the application. By externalizing the logging configuration, a developer can make the logging work locally by configuring logs to go to a file or to the console. Later on, when the application is deployed to a production server, the administrator can configure the log appender to be something else, such as the ELK stack we are going to discuss later. This way, the code doesn't need to be changed, and we can modify the behavior and destination of the logging at deployment time.

An application server such as WildFly offers its own configuration system that plugs in to the log4j system.

If you don't use an application server, newer versions of log4j support many different configuration formats. Here is an XML-style file, which will look for `log4j2-test.xml` in the classpath:

```xml
<?xml version="1.0" encoding="UTF-8"?>
<Configuration status="WARN">
  <Appenders>
    <Console name="Console" target="SYSTEM_OUT">
      <PatternLayout pattern="%d{HH:mm:ss.SSS} [%t] %-5level
%logger{36} - %msg%n"/>
    </Console>
  </Appenders>
  <Loggers>
    <Root level="error">
      <AppenderRef ref="Console"/>
    </Root>
  </Loggers>
</Configuration>
```

The ELK stack

The ELK stack consists of the following components:

- **Logstash**: This is an open source logging framework similar to log4j. The server component of Logstash processes incoming logs.

- **Elasticsearch**: This stores all of the logs and indexes them, as the name implies, for searching.

- **Kibana**: This is the web interface for the searching and visualization of logs.

To see how it works, we will follow a log message all the way from where it originates inside the code, through the intermediary network layers, to the end destination at the network operator's screen:

1. Deep down in the code, a Java exception occurs. The application unexpectedly can't map a user ID present in an import file to the user IDs in the database. The following error is logged with log4j:

    ```
    logger.error("cant find imported user id in database")
    ```

2. The log4j system is configured to log errors to a Logstash backend, as follows:

    ```
    log4j.appender.applog=org.apache.log4j.net.SocketAppender
    log4j.appender.applog.port=5000
    log4j.appender.applog.remoteHost=master
    log4j.appender.applog.DatePattern='.'yyyy-MM-dd
    log4j.appender.applog.layout=org.apache.log4j.PatternLayout
    log4j.appender.applog.layout.ConversionPattern=%d %-5p [%t] %c %M
    - %m%n
    log4j.rootLogger=warn, applog
    log4j.logger.nl=debug
    ```

3. The Logstash system is configured as follows to listen to the ports described by the log4j system. The Logstash daemon must be started separately from your application as shown:

    ```
    input {
       log4j {
         mode => server
         host => "0.0.0.0"
         port => 5000
         type => "log4j"
       }
    }
    output {
    stdout { codec => rubydebug }
    stdout { }
      elasticsearch {
        cluster => "elasticsearch"
      }
    }
    ```

4. The Elasticsearch engine receives the log output and makes it searchable.

5. The administrator can open the Kibana GUI application and watch the log appear in real time or also search for historical data.

You might think that this is a lot of complexity, and you would be correct. But it's interesting to note that log4j can be configured to support this complex scenario as well as much simpler scenarios, so you can't really go wrong using log4j or one of its compatible competitors.

You can start out with not using any network logging and just use plain log files. This is good enough for many situations. If and when you need the extra power of the ELK stack, you can add it later. It is useful to keep the log files around as well. If the advanced logging facilities fail for some reason, you can always resort to using the traditional Unix `grep` utility on the log files.

Kibana has many features to help you analyze your log data. You can graph the data and filter log data for the particular patterns that you are looking for.

To try all of this out in practice, we can use the official Kibana and Elasticsearch Docker images available on Docker Hub:

```
docker run -d elasticsearch &&
docker run --link some-elasticsearch:elasticsearch -d kibana
```

If all goes well, we will be able to access the Kibana user interface, which looks like this:

Summary

In this chapter, we had a look at some of the many options available for monitoring our deployed code: Nagios to monitor the states of hosts and services; Munin, Ganglia, and Graphite to graph statistics from our hosts; and log4j and the ELK stack to keep track of log information.

In the next chapter, we will look at tools that help with workflows within the development organization, such as issue trackers.

9

Issue Tracking

In the previous chapter, we looked at how we can keep an eye on our deployed code with monitoring and log handling solutions.

In this chapter, we will look at systems that handle development workflows within an organization, such as issue tracking software. Such systems are an important aid while implementing Agile processes.

What are issue trackers used for?

From an Agile process standpoint, issue trackers are used to help with the minutiae and details of the Agile process. The entities handled by the issue tracker might represent work items, bugs, and issues. Most Agile processes include an idea of how to manage tasks that an Agile team are to perform, in the form of Post-it notes on a board or an electronic equivalent.

When working in an Agile setting, it is common to have a board with issues on handwritten Post-it notes. This is a central concept in the Kanban method, since Kanban actually means *signboard* in Japanese. The board gives a nice overview of the work in progress and is pretty easy to manage because you just move the Post-it notes around on the board to represent state changes in the workflow.

It is also pretty easy to change your Kanban board by just rewriting the various markers, such as lanes, that you have written on your board:

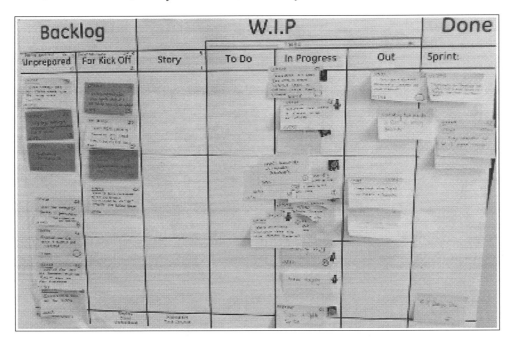

Physical boards are also common with Scrum teams.

On the other hand, computerized issue trackers, which are mostly web-based, offer much better detail and can be used when working remotely. These issue trackers also help you remember steps in your process, among other benefits.

Ideally, one would like both a physical board and an issue tracker, but it is a lot of work to keep them synchronized. There is no easy way to solve this basic contention. Some people use a projector to show the issue tracker as if it was a board, but it does not have the same tactile feel to it, and gathering around a projected image or monitor is not the same thing as gathering around a physical board. Boards also have the advantage of being always available and convenient for reference when team members want to discuss tasks.

Technically, issue trackers are usually implemented as databases of objects representing state machines, with various degrees of sophistication. You create an issue with a web interface or by other means, such as e-mail or automation; then, the issue goes through various states due to human interaction, and in the end, the issue is archived in a closed state for future reference. Sometimes, the flow progresses due to an interaction from another system. A simple example might be that a task is no longer deemed valid because it is overdue and is automatically closed.

Some examples of workflows and issues

Although the term "issue" is used throughout this chapter, some systems use the terms "ticket" or "bug". Technically, they are the same thing. An issue might also represent a to-do item, enhancement request, or any other type of work item. It might feel slightly counterintuitive that, technically, an enhancement is basically the same thing as a bug, but if you see the enhancement as a missing feature, it starts to make sense.

An issue has various metadata associated with it, depending on what it represents and what the issue tracker supports. The most basic type of issue is very simple, yet useful. It has the following basic attributes:

- **Description**: This is a free-form textual description of the issue
- **Reporter**: This represents the person who opened the issue
- **Assigned**: This is the person who should work on the item.

Also, it has two states: open and closed.

This is usually the minimum that an issue tracker provides. If you compare this with a Post-it note, the only extra metadata is the reporter, and you could probably remove that as well and the tracker would still be functional. With a Post-it note, you handle open and closed states simply by putting the Post-it on the board or removing it.

When project managers first encounter an electronic issue tracker, there is often a tendency to go completely overboard with adding complexity to the state machines and attribute storage of the tracker. That said, there is clearly a lot of useful information that can be added to an issue tracker without overdoing it.

Apart from the previously mentioned basic information, these additional attributes are usually quite useful:

- **Due date**: The date on which the issue is expected to be resolved.

- **Milestone**: A milestone is a way to group issues together in useful work packages that are larger than a single issue. A milestone can represent the output from a Scrum sprint, for example. A milestone usually also has a due date, and if you use the milestone feature, the due dates on individual issues are normally not used.

- **Attachments**: It might be convenient to be able to attach screenshots and documents to an issue, which might be useful for the developer working on the issue or the tester verifying it.

- **Work estimates**: It can be useful to have an estimate of the expected work expenditure required to resolve the issue. This can be used for planning purposes. Likewise, a field with the actual time spent on the issue can also be useful for various calculations. On the other hand, it is always tricky to do estimates, and in the end, it might be more trouble than it's worth. Many teams do quite well without this type of information in their issue tracker.

The following are also some useful states that can be used to model an Agile workflow better than the plain open and closed states. The open and closed states are repeated here for clarity:

- **Open**: The issue is reported, and no one is working on it as of yet

- **In progress**: Somebody is assigned to the issue and working on resolving it

- **Ready for test**: The issue is completed and is now ready for verification. It is unassigned again

- **Testing**: Someone is assigned to work on testing the implementation of the issue

- **Done**: The task is marked as ready and unassigned once more. The done state is used to mark issues to keep track of them until the end of a sprint, for example, if the team is working with the Scrum method

- **Closed**: The issue is no longer monitored, but it is still kept around for reference

In the best case scenario, issues progress from one state to the next in an orderly fashion. In a more realistic scenario, there is a likelihood that a task goes from testing to open instead of done, since testing might reveal that the issue wasn't really properly fixed.

What do we need from an issue tracker?

What do we need from an issue tracker apart from it supporting the basic workflows described previously? There are many concerns, some of them not immediately apparent. Some things to consider are listed as follows:

- What scale do we need?

  Most tools work well on scales of up to about 20 people, but beyond that, we need to consider performance and licensing requirements. How many issues do we need to be able to track? How many users need access to the issue tracker? These are some of the questions we might have.

- How many licenses do we need?

  In this regard, free software gains the upper hand, because proprietary software can have unintuitive pricing. Free software can be free of charge, with optional support licensing.

  Most of the issue trackers mentioned in this chapter are free software, with the exception of Jira.

- Are there performance limitations?

  Performance is not usually a limiting factor, since most trackers use a production-ready database such as PostgreSQL or MariaDB as the backend database. Most issue trackers described in this chapter behave well at the scales usually associated with an organization's in-house issue tracker. Bugzilla has been proven in installations that handle a large number of issues and face the public Internet.

  Nevertheless, it is good practice to evaluate the performance of the systems you intend to deploy. Perhaps some peculiarity of your intended use triggers some performance issue. An example might be that most issue trackers use a relational database as a backend, and relational databases are not the best for representing hierarchical tree structures if one needs to do recursive queries. In normal use cases, this is not a problem, but if you intend to use deeply nested trees of issues on a large scale, problems might surface.

- What support options are available, and what quality are they?

  It is hard to determine the quality of support before actually using it, but here are some ideas to help with evaluation:

  - For open source projects, support is dependent on the size of the user community. Also, there often are commercial support providers available.

  - Commercial issue trackers can have both paid and community support.

- Can we use an issue tracker hosted off-site or not?

  There are many companies that host issue trackers. These include Atlassian's Jira tracker, which can both be installed on customer premises or hosted by Atlassian. Another example of a hosted issue tracker is Trello from Trello, Inc.

  Deploying issue trackers in your own network is usually not very hard. They are among the simpler of the systems described in this book with regard to installation complexity. Normally, you need a database backend and a web application backend layer. Usually, the hardest part is getting integration with authentication servers and mail servers to work. Nevertheless, even if hosting your own issue tracker installation isn't really hard, there is no denying that using a hosted tracker is easier.

  Some organizations can't leak data about their work outside their own networks for legal or other reasons. For these organizations, hosted issue trackers are not an option. They must deploy issue trackers inside their own networks.

- Does the issue workflow system adapt to our needs?

  Some systems, such as Jira, allow highly flexible state machines to define the flow and integrated editors to edit it. Others have more minimalistic flows. The right solution for you depends on your needs. Some people start out with wanting a very complex flow and wind up realizing they only need the open and closed states. Others realize they need complex flows to support the complexities of their process.

  A configurable flow is useful in large organizations, because it can encapsulate knowledge about processes that might not be readily apparent. For instance, when a bug has been squashed, Mike in the quality assurance department should verify the fix. This is not so useful in a small organization, because everyone knows what to do anyway. However, in a large organization, the opposite is often true. It is useful to get some help in deciding who should take care of a task next and what to do.

- Does the issue tracker support our choice of the Agile method?

  Most issue trackers mentioned in this chapter have underlying data models flexible enough to represent any sort of Agile process. All you really need, in a sense, is a configurable state machine. Issue trackers might, of course, add additional features to provide better support for particular Agile methods and workflows.

  These extra features that support Agile methods usually boil down to two primary classes: visualization and reporting. While these are nice to have, my opinion is that too much focus is placed on these features, especially by inexperienced team leaders. Visualization and reporting do add value, but not as much as one might believe at the outset.

   Keep this in mind when selecting features for your issue tracker. Make sure that you will actually use that impressive report you have been wanting.

- Does the system integrate easily with other systems in our organization?

  Examples of systems that an issue tracker might integrate with include code repositories, single sign on, e-mail systems, and so on. A broken build might cause the build server to automatically generate a ticket in the issue tracker and assign it to the developer that broke the build, for example.

  Since we are primarily concerned with development workflows here, the main integration we need is with the code repository system. Most of the issue trackers we explore here have some form of integration with a code repository system.

- Is the tracker extendable?

  It is often useful for an issue tracker to have some form of API as an extension point. APIs can be used to integrate to other systems and also customize the tracker so that it fits our organization's processes.

  Perhaps you need an HTML-formatted display of currently open issues to show on a publicly viewable monitor. This can be accomplished with a good API. Perhaps you want the issue tracker to trigger deploys in your deployment system. This can also be accomplished with a good issue tracker API.

  A good API opens up many possibilities that would otherwise be closed for us.

- Does the tracker offer multi-project support?

  If you have many teams and projects, it might be useful to have separate issue trackers for each project. Thus, a useful feature of an issue tracker is to be able to partition itself into several subprojects, each having an isolated issue tracker inside the system.

  As usual, trade-offs are involved. If you have many separate issue trackers, how do you move an issue from one tracker to another? This is needed when you have several teams working on different sets of tasks; for instance, development teams and quality assurance teams. From a DevOps perspective, it is not good if the tools pull the teams further apart rather than bringing them closer together.

  So, while it is good for each team to have its own issue tracker within the main system, there should also be good support for handling all the tasks of several teams together as a whole.

- Does the issue tracker support multiple clients?

  While not usually a feature deemed as a critical acceptance requirement for choosing an issue tracker, it can be convenient to access the issue tracker via multiple clients and interfaces. It is very convenient for developers to be able to access the issue tracker while working inside their integrated development environment, for instance.

  Some organizations that work with free software prefer a completely e-mail based workflow, such as Debian's debugs. Such requirements are rare in an enterprise setting, though.

Problems with issue tracker proliferation

As it is technically very easy to set up an issue tracker these days, it often happens that teams set up their own issue trackers to handle their own issues and tasks. It happens for many other types of tools such as editors, but editors are among the personal tools of a developer, and their primary use case isn't the sharing of collaboration surfaces with other people. Issue tracker proliferation is therefore a problem, while editor proliferation isn't.

A contributing cause of the issue tracker proliferation problem is that a large organization might standardize a type of tracker that few actually like to use. A typical reason is that only the needs of one type of team, such as the quality assurance team or the operations team, is being considered while deciding on an issue tracker. Another reason is that only a limited amount of licenses were bought for the issue tracker, and the rest of the team will have to make do on their own.

It is also quite common that the developers use one kind of tracker, the quality assurance team another, and the operations team yet another completely different and incompatible system.

So, while it is suboptimal for the organization as a whole to have many different issue tracker systems that do the same thing, it might be perceived as a win for a team that gets to choose its own tools in this area.

Again, one of the central ideas in DevOps is to bring different teams and roles closer together. Proliferation of mutually incompatible collaboration tools is not helpful in this regard. This mostly happens in large organizations, and there is usually no simple solution to the problem.

If you use a free software tracker, you at least get rid of the limited license problem. Finding a system that pleases everyone in every regard is, of course, much harder. It might help to limit the scope of selection criteria so that rather than the management, the issue tracker tool pleases the people who will actually be using it all day long. This usually also means putting less focus on reporting spiffy burn down charts and more on actually getting things done.

All the trackers

Next, we will explore a selection of different issue tracker systems. They are all easy to try out before you commit to an actual deployment. Most are free, but some proprietary alternatives are also mentioned.

All the trackers mentioned here are present on the comparison page on Wikipedia at `https://en.wikipedia.org/wiki/Comparison_of_issue-tracking_systems`.

Since we can only explore a selection of issue trackers, the following were chosen because they exhibit differences due to different design choices. Bugzilla was designed for large-scale public-facing trackers. Trac was designed for simplicity and tool integration. Redmine as a fully featured project management tool with an issue tracker. The GitLab tracker was chosen for simplicity, and Git integration and Jira for usability.

We begin our issue tracker exploration with Bugzilla, since it is one of the earliest issue trackers and is still popular. This means that its flows are pretty mature since they have proven themselves over a long period of time.

Bugzilla

Bugzilla can be said to be the grandfather of all the issue tracker systems described in this chapter. Bugzilla has been around since 1998 and is in use by many high-profile organizations, such as Red Hat, the Linux kernel project, and the Mozilla project. If you have ever reported a bug for one of these products, you have likely already encountered Bugzilla.

Bugzilla is free software maintained by the Mozilla project, which also produces the well-known Firefox browser. Bugzilla is written in Perl.

Bugzilla focuses, unsurprisingly, on tracking bugs rather than handling other issue types. Handling other types of tasks, such as providing a wiki, needs to be done separately.

Many organizations use Bugzilla as a public-facing tool where issues can be reported. As a result, Bugzilla has good security features.

There is a demonstration installation where one can test the latest features of the development version of Bugzilla at `https://landfill.bugzilla.org/bugzilla-tip/`.

Bugzilla supports customizations. It is possible to add custom fields to issues and customize the workflow.

Bugzilla has both the XML-RPC and JSON REST APIs.

Since Bugzilla has been around for a long time, there are many extensions and plugins available, including alternative clients.

The following figure shows the Bugzilla bug state machine, or workflow:

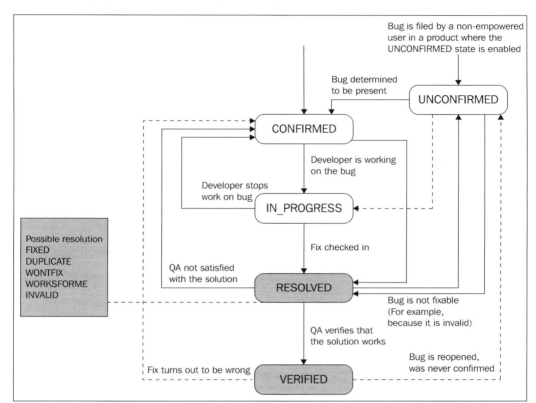

This workflow is configurable, but the default states are as follows:

- **Unconfirmed**: A new bug by a non-powered user begins in the unconfirmed state

- **Confirmed**: If the bug is confirmed to be worthy of investigation, it is put in the confirmed state

- **In progress**: When a developer starts working on resolving the bug, the in progress state is used

- **Resolved**: When developers believe that they have finished fixing the bug, they put it in the resolved state

- **Verified**: When the quality assurance team agrees that the bug is fixed, it is put in the verified state

Let's try out Bugzilla now.

There are several Docker hub images available for Bugzilla, and it is most likely also available in the repositories of your Linux distribution.

This starts Bugzilla in a separate container, complete with a suitable MySQL configuration. The port is arbitrarily chosen:

```
docker run -p 6050:80 dklawren/docker-bugzilla
```

Try accessing the interface now, at `http://localhost:6050`.

You will be greeted by this view:

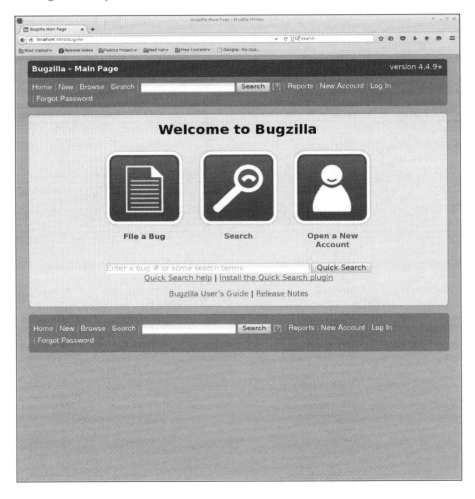

Bugzilla requires you to have an account in order to submit bugs. You can either use the administrator account or make a new one.

You can log in using the administrator username admin@bugzilla.org, and the password is initially password. Now see the following steps to create and resolve a bug:

1. Choose **Open a New Account**. This will prompt you for your e-mail address. A confirmation mail with a link will be sent to the address. Ensure the port number is correct in the link; otherwise, create it. Your account should be created now.

2. Try creating a new bug with the **File a Bug** option. Bugzilla needs you to provide the product and component for the bug. There is a **TestProduct** and **TestComponent** option available; we can use them to report our bug:

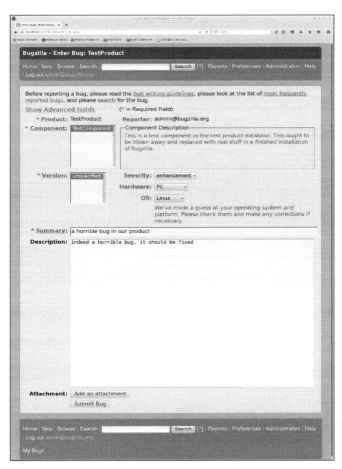

3. Now that the bug is open, we can comment on it. Every time we comment on a bug, we can also move it to a new state, depending on our access level. Try adding some comments as shown in the following screenshot:

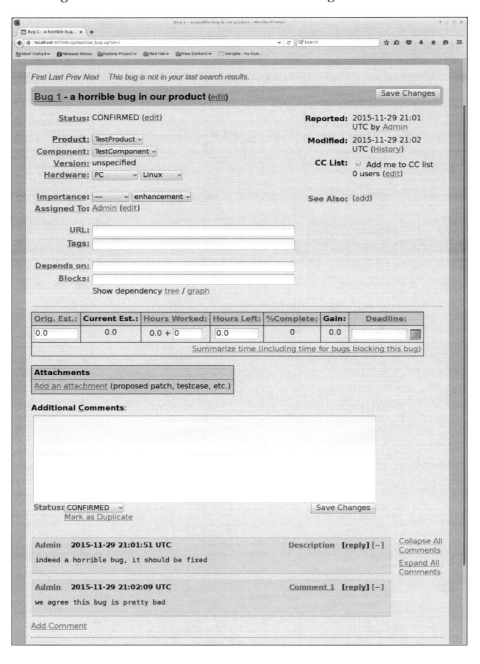

4. Try searching for the bug. There is a simple search page and an advanced one. The advanced page is depicted in the following screenshot. It lets you search for most field combinations:

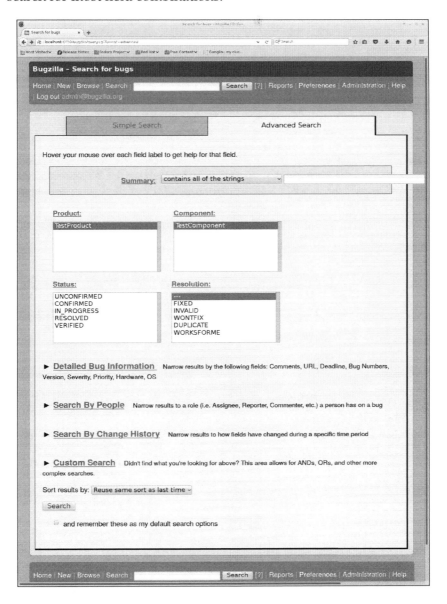

5. Eventually, when you are done, mark the bug as resolved.

As you can see, Bugzilla has all the features that can be expected from an issue tracker. It is geared towards a workflow that is optimized for working on a large number of bugs in a number of products and components. It is fairly easy to get started with Bugzilla if you are content with how it works out of the box. Customization requires some additional effort.

Trac

Trac is an issue tracker that is fairly easy to set up and test. The main attraction of Trac is that it is small and integrates a number of systems together in one concise model. Trac was one of the earliest issue trackers that showed that an issue tracker, a wiki, and a repository viewer could be beneficially integrated together.

Trac is written in Python and published under a free software license by Edgewall. It was originally licensed under the GPL, but since 2005, it has been licensed under a BSD-style license.

Trac is highly configurable through the use of a plugin architecture. There are many plugins available, a number of which are listed on `https://trac-hacks.org`.

Trac develops at a conservative pace, which many users are quite happy with. Trac also has an XML-RPC API, which can be used to read and modify issues.

Trac traditionally used to integrate only with Subversion, but now features Git support.

Trac also has an integrated wiki feature, which makes it a fairly complete system.

There are several Docker hub Trac images available, and Trac is also usually available in the repositories of Linux distributions.

There is a Dockerfile for Trac available in this book's code bundle, which we can also use. Take a look at the following command:

```
docker run -d -p 6051:8080 barogi/trac:1.0.2
```

This will make a Trac instance available on `port 6051`. Let's try it out:

- Accessing `http://localhost:6051/` shows a list of available projects. At the outset, only the default project is available.

- The menu row at the right shows the basic features available by default, as can be seen in this screenshot:

- **Wiki** is a traditional wiki, where you can write documents useful for development, for instance.

- **Timeline** will show events that have occurred in Trac:

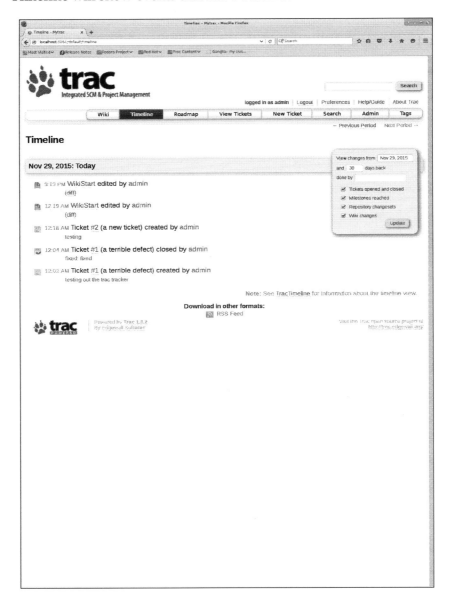

- **Roadmap** will show tickets organized into milestones:

- **View Tickets,** as the name implies, shows tickets. There are several possible reports, and you can create new ones. This is a very useful feature that lets different teams and roles see the information that is relevant to them:

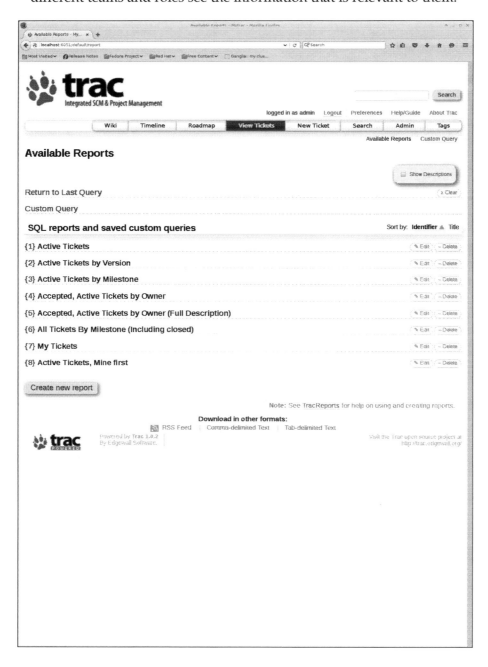

Now, try logging in with both the username and password as `admin`.

You now get a new menu bar entry called **New Ticket**. Try creating a ticket. As you type, a live preview will be updated in the lower part of the window:

The ticket is now in the "new" state. We can change the state with the **Modify** button. Try resolving the ticket and commenting on it. The next state will be "closed".

Since one of the main selling points of Trac is the tight integration of a Wiki, issue tracker, and repository, let's try the integration out. Edit the main Wiki page. Trac uses a simple wiki syntax. Create a new heading, using an equals sign to mark it as shown in the following screenshot:

When we submit the changes, the issue identifier becomes clickable, and we can visit the issue.

If you mention a bug in the commit message of a code change, Trac will make it clickable as well in its changeset browser. This is a simple and convenient feature inspired by wikis.

The Admin interface allows customization of the Trac instance. You can manage many of the entities in Trac directly in the interface, but it's not possible to manage every aspect of Trac from here. You need to configure some of the following aspects in the filesystem:

- Users
- Components
- Milestones
- Priorities
- Resolutions
- Severity
- Ticket types

Trac has a configurable state machine. By default, new installations get a state machine only slightly more complex than the minimal open/closed state machine. The state machine is as follows:

- New
- Assigned
- Accepted

- Closed
- Reopened

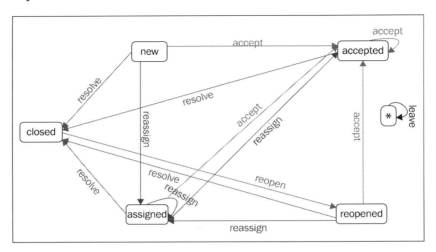

The Trac distribution comes with a set of example workflow configurations in the form of .ini files that describe workflow states and transitions. It's not possible to edit the workflow in the GUI at present.

This concludes our look at the Trac issue tracker. It is attractive, if you like the simplicity and tool integration.

Redmine

Redmine is a popular issue tracker written in Ruby on Rails. Its design shares many similarities with Trac.

Redmine has two forks as well: ChiliProject and OpenProject. While ChiliProject's development has stalled, OpenProject continues to be developed.

Redmine is free software. It is similar to Trac in the sense that it integrates several tools together into a coherent whole. It is also web based, like the other issue trackers we explore here.

Redmine has a number of additional features when compared with the out-of-the-box experience of Trac. Some of them are as follows:

- Multiple projects can be managed from within the web interface
- Gantt charts and calendars can be used

There is a Dockerfile for Redmine available in this book's code bundle, and there is also an official Redmine image available at the Docker hub. Take a look at this command:

```
docker run -d -p  6052:3000 redmine
```

This will start a Redmine instance available on the host `port 6052`. This instance will use a SQLite database, so it will not scale to production usage. You can configure the Redmine container to use a Postgres or MariaDB container as a database if and when you decide to do a production installation.

You can log in with the default username and password, both `admin`.

You need to initialize the database manually before proceeding. Use the **Administration** link at the top of the page. Follow the instructions on the page:

You can create a new project from within the user interface. If you don't follow the previous database initialization step first, the new project will not have the necessary configuration, and you won't be able to create issues. Redmine's **New project** view is included in the screenshot below:

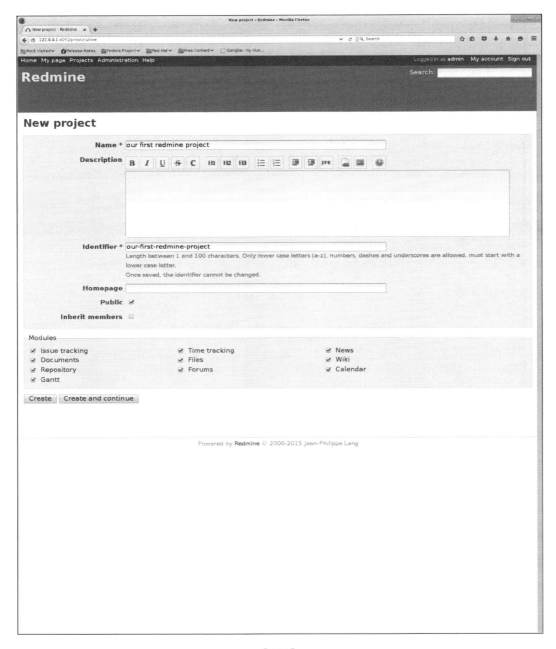

Now that we have created a project, we can now create an issue. With Redmine, you choose a class for your issue: by default, **Bug**, **Feature**, and **Support**. Let's make a new feature issue:

There is also a **Gantt** view and a **Calendar** view, among many other features.

Here is the **Gantt** view:

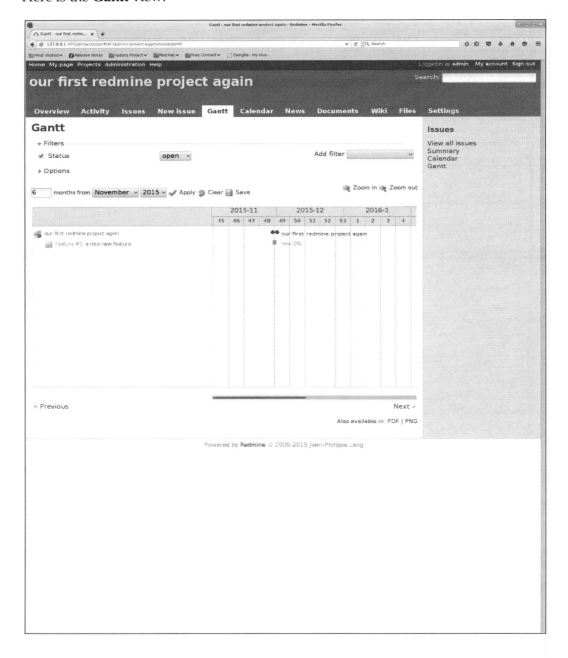

And here is the **Calendar** view:

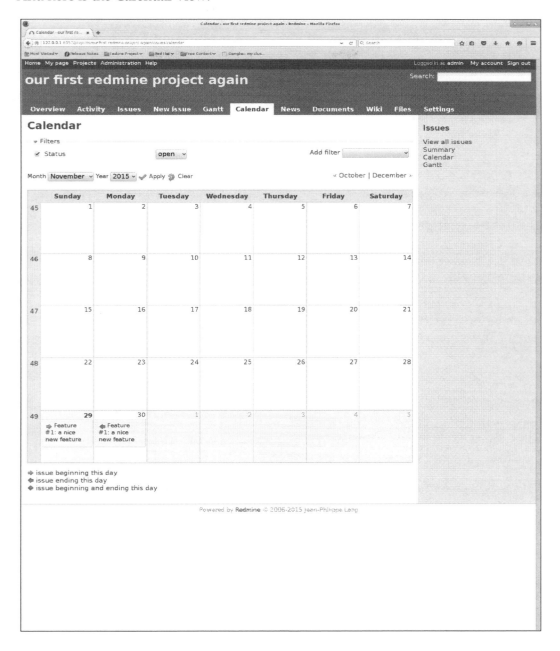

A Redmine issue has the following default state machine:

- New
- In Progress
- Resolved
- Feedback
- Closed
- Rejected

In conclusion, Redmine is a nice tracker that has many nice features and builds on the experience from Trac.

The GitLab issue tracker

GitLab's issue tracker is, as one might expect, very well integrated with the Git repository management system. GitLab's issue tracker is nice looking but is not, at the time of writing, very flexible. It might be deemed good enough for teams that prefer simplicity in their tools.

GitLab has a quick development pace, so the feature set might be expected to change. The GitLab issue tracker tracks issues per repository, so if you have many repositories, it might be difficult to get an overview of all the issues at the same time.

The suggested solution for this concern is creating a separate project where issues concerning several repositories are gathered.

While the GitLab issue tracker lacks many of the features seen in competing systems, it does have a nice, flexible API, and there is a command-line client for the API, so you can try it out from the convenience of your shell.

Testing the GitLab API is quite easy:

First, install the GitLab CLI

Then, set the following two environment variables that describe the endpoint of the GitLab API and the authorization token:

- `GITLAB_API_PRIVATE_TOKEN` = *<token from your project>*
- `GITLAB_API_ENDPOINT` = `http://gitlab.matangle.com:50003/api/v3`

Now you can list issues and so on. There is an inbuilt help system:

```
gitlab help Issues
+--------------+
|    Issues    |
+--------------+
| close_issue  |
+--------------+
| create_issue |
+--------------+
| edit_issue   |
+--------------+
| issue        |
+--------------+
| issues       |
+--------------+
| reopen_issue |
+--------------+
```

GitLab issues only have two conventional states: open and closed. This is pretty spartan, but the idea is to instead use other types of metadata, such as labels, to describe issues. A GitLab issue tracker label is made up of text and a background color that can be associated with an issue. More than one label can be associated.

There is also the possibility of embedding a to-do list in the Markdown format in the issue description. While labels and to-do lists can together be used to create flexible views, this does not really allow for the traditional use case of issue tracker state machines. You have to remember what you need to do yourself: the GitLab issue tracker does not help you remember process flows. Small teams might find the lack of ceremony in the GitLab tracker refreshing, and it's certainly easy to set up once you have already set up GitLab—you get it installed already.

The user interface is quite intuitive. Here is the **Create Issue** view:

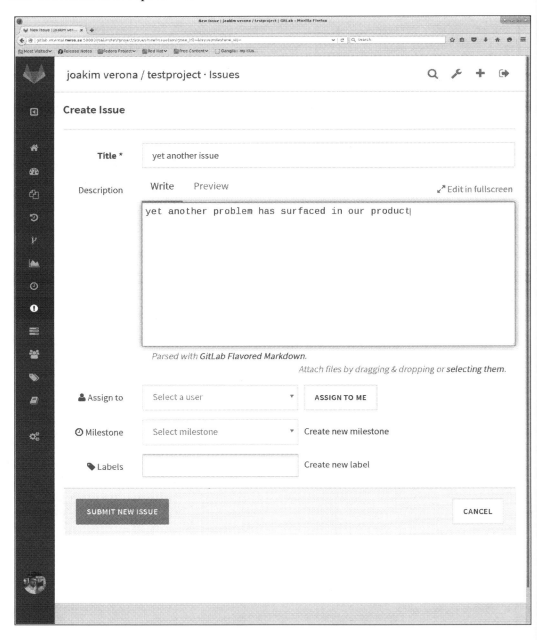

Here are some of the features of the interface:

- **Assign to**: People who can be assigned as members of the project.
- **Labels**: You can have a default set of labels, create your own, or mix. Here are the default labels:
  - **Bug**
  - **Confirmed**
  - **Critical**
  - **Discussion**
  - **Documentation**
  - **Enhancement**
  - **Suggestion**
  - **Support**

Here are some of the attributes that can be used for an issue:

- **Milestones**: You can group issues together in milestones. The milestones describe when issues are to be closed in a timeline fashion.
- **GitLab Flavored Markdown support**: GitLab supports Markdown and some extra markup that makes linking together different entities in GitLab easier.
- **Attach files**

After the complexity of the Bugzilla, Trac, and Redmine interfaces, the no-nonsense approach of the GitLab issue tracker can feel quite refreshing!

Jira

Jira is a flexible bug tracker by Atlassian, written in Java. It is the only proprietary issue tracker reviewed here.

While I prefers **FLOSS (Free/Libre/Open Source Software)**, Jira is very adaptable and free of charge for small teams of up to 15 people. Unlike Trac and GitLab, the different modules such as the wiki and repository viewer are separate products. If you need a Wiki, you deploy one separately, and Atlassian's own Confluence Wiki is the one that integrates with the least amount of friction. Atlassian also provides a code browser called **Fisheye** for code repository integration and browsing.

For small teams, Jira licensing is cheap, but it quickly becomes more expensive.

By default, Jira's workflow is much like the Bugzilla workflow:

- Open
- In Progress
- Resolved
- Closed
- Reopened

There are several Docker Hub images available; one is `cptactionhank/atlassian-jira`—but please remember, Jira is not free software.

Let's try Jira now:

```
docker run -p 6053:8080 cptactionhank/atlassian-jira:latest
```

You can access the interface on `port 6053`. Jira is somewhat more convoluted to try out, because you need to create an Atlassian account before starting. Log in with your account when you are done.

Jira starts out with a simple tutorial, where you create a project and an issue in the project. If you follow along, the resulting view will look like this:

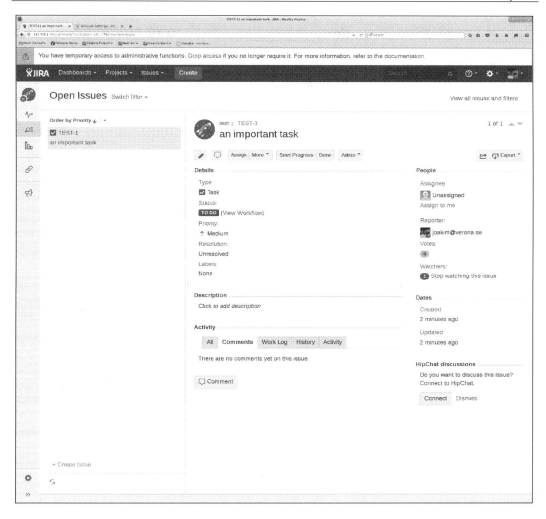

Jira has many features, many of them available through plugins available in an inbuilt app store. If you can live with Jira not being free software, it is probably the issue tracker with the glossiest look of those reviewed here. It is also fairly complex to configure and administer.

Summary

In this chapter, we looked at various systems that can implement issue tracking workflow support in our organization. As usual, there are many solutions to choose from, especially in this area, where the tools are of the type that are used every day.

The next chapter will deal with something slightly more esoteric: DevOps and the Internet of Things.

10
The Internet of Things and DevOps

In the previous chapter, we explored some of the many different tool options, such as issue trackers, available to us to help us manage workflows.

This chapter will be forward looking: how can DevOps assist us in the emerging field of the Internet of Things?

The Internet of Things, or IoT for short, presents challenges for DevOps. We will explore what these challenges are.

Since IoT is not a clearly defined term, we will begin with some background.

Introducing the IoT and DevOps

The phrase **Internet of Things** was coined in the late 1990s, allegedly by the British entrepreneur Kevin Ashton, while he was working with RFID technology. Kevin became interested in using RFID to manage supply chains while working at Proctor and Gamble.

RFID, or **Radio Frequency ID**, is the technology behind the little tags you wear on your key chain and use to open doors, for instance. RFID tags are an example of interesting things that can, indirectly in this case, be connected to the Internet. RFID tags are not limited to opening doors, of course, and the form factor does not have to be limited to a tag on a key chain.

An RFID tag contains a small chip, about 2 millimeters squared, and a coil. When placed near a reader, the coil is charged with electricity by induction, and the chip is given power long enough for it to transmit a unique identifier to the reader's hardware. The reader, in turn, sends the tag's identification string to a server that decides, for example, whether it is going to open the lock associated with the reader or not. The server is likely connected to the Internet so that the identifiers associated with the RFID tags can be added or deleted remotely depending on changing circumstances regarding who has access to the locked door. Several different systems work in symbiosis to achieve the desired outcome.

Other interesting IoT technologies include passive QR codes that can be scanned by a camera and provide information to a system. The newer Bluetooth low energy technology provides intelligent active sensors. Such sensors can operate up to a year on a lithium cell.

Below, two RFID tags for operating locks are depicted:

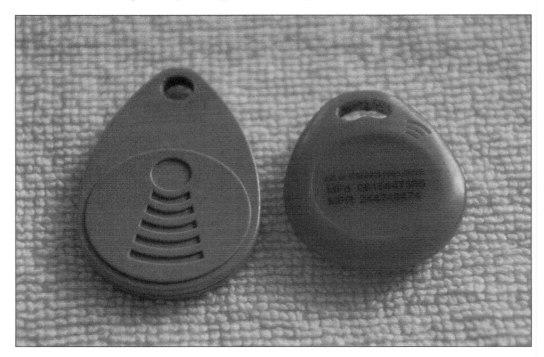

The term "Internet of Things" is pretty vague. When is it a "thing" and when is it a computer? Or is it a little bit of both?

Let's take a small computer, such as the Raspberry Pi; it is a **System on a Chip (SoC)**, mounted on a board the size of a credit card. It's small, but is still a full computer and powerful enough to run Java application servers, web servers, and Puppet agents.

Compared to traditional computers, IoT devices are constrained in various ways. Often, they are embedded devices that are placed in difficult-to-access, constrained locations. This, then, would seem to be the defining characteristic of the IoT from a DevOps point of view: the devices might be constrained in different regards. We cannot use every technique that we use on servers or desktop machines. The constraints could be limited memory, processing power, or access, to name a few.

Here are some example types of IoT devices, which you have probably either encountered already or soon will:

- **Smartwatches**: Today, a smartwatch can have a Bluetooth and Wi-Fi connection and automatically detect available upgrades. It can download new firmware and upgrade itself on user interaction. There are many smartwatches available today, from the robust Pebble to Android Wear and Apple Watch. There already are smartwatches with mobile network connections as well, and eventually, they will become commonplace.

- **Keyboards**: A keyboard can have upgradeable firmware. A keyboard is actually a good example of an IoT device, in a sense. It provides many sensors. It can run software that provides sensor readouts to more powerful machines that in the end are Internet-connected. There are fully programmable keyboards with open firmware, such as the Ergodox, which interfaces an Arduino-style board to a keyboard matrix (http://ergodox.org/).

- **Home automation systems**: These are Internet-connected and can be controlled with smartphones or desktop computers. The Telldus TellStick is an example of such a device that lets you control remote power relays via an Internet-connected device. There are many other similar systems.

- **Wireless surveillance cameras**: These can be monitored with a smartphone interface. There are many providers for different market segments, such as Axis Communications.

- **Biometric sensors**: Such sensors include fitness sensors, for example, pulse meters, body scales, and accelerometers placed on the body. The Withings body scale measures biometrics and uploads it to a server and allows you to read statistics through a website. There are accelerometers in smartwatches and phones as well that keep track of your movements.

- **Bluetooth-based key finders**: You can activate these from your smartphone if you lose your keys.

- **Car computers**: These do everything from handling media and navigation to management of physical control systems in the car, such as locks, windows, and doors.

- **Audio and video systems**: These include entertainment systems, such as networked audio players, and video streaming hardware, such as Google Chromecast and Apple TV.

- **Smartphones**: The ubiquitous smartphones are really small computers with 3G or 4G modems and Wi-Fi that connects them to the wider Internet.

- **Wi-Fi capable computers embedded in memory cards**: These make it possible to convert an existing DSLR camera into a Wi-Fi capable camera that can automatically upload images to a server.

- **Network routers in homes or offices**: These are in fact, small servers that often can be upgraded remotely from the ISP side.

- **Networked printers**: These are pretty intelligent these days and can interact with cloud services for easier printing from many different devices.

The list can, of course, go on, and all of these devices are readily available and used in many households today.

It is interesting to note that many of the devices mentioned are very similar from a technical viewpoint, even if they are used for completely different purposes. Most smartphones use variants of the ARM CPU architecture, which can be licensed across manufacturers together with a few variants of peripheral chips. MIPS processors are popular among router hardware vendors and Atmel RISC processors among embedded hardware implementers, for example.

The basic ARM chips are available to developers and hobbyists alike for easy prototyping. The Raspberry Pi is ARM-based and can be used as a prototyping device for professional use. Arduino similarly makes Atmel-architecture devices available for easy prototyping of hardware.

This makes a perfect storm of IoT innovation possible:

- The devices are cheap and easy to acquire even in small runs.

- The devices are simple to develop for and get prototyping platforms

- The development environments are similar, which makes them easier to learn. A lot of the time, the GNU Compiler Collection, or GCC, is used.

- There is a lot of support available in forums, mailing lists, documentation, and so on.

For powerful devices such as the Raspberry Pi, we can use the same methods and practices that we use for servers. Pi devices can be servers, just less powerful than a traditional server. For IoT devices, agentless deployment systems are a better fit than systems that require an agent.

Tinier devices, such as the Atmel embedded CPUs used in Arduinos, are more constrained. Typically, you compile new firmware and deploy them to the device during reboot, when special bootstrap loader code runs. The device then connects to the host via USB.

During development, one can automate the upload of firmware by connecting a separate device that resets the original device and puts it into loader mode. This might work during development, but it's not cost-effective in a real deployment scenario since it affects costs. These are the types of problems that might affect DevOps when working with the IoT. In the development environment, we might be able to use, more or less, the methods that we are used to from developing server applications, perhaps with some extra hardware. From a quality assurance perspective, though, there is a risk involved in deploying on hardware that is different to that used in testing.

The future of the IoT according to the market

According to the research group Gartner, there will be approximately 6.4 billion things connected to the Internet at the end of 2016: a 30 percent increase since 2015. Further away, at the end of the year 2020, there will be an estimated 21 billion Internet-connected devices. The consumer market will be responsible for the greatest number of devices, and enterprises for the greatest spending.

The next generation of wireless networks, which are tentatively called 5G mobile networks, is expected to reach the market in 2020, which isn't too far away at the time of writing. The upcoming mobile networks will have capabilities suitable for IoT devices and even be way ahead of today's 4G networks.

Some of the projected abilities of the new mobile network standards include:

- The ability to connect many more devices than what is possible with today's networks. This will enable the deployment of massive sensor networks with hundreds of thousands of sensors.
- Data rates of several tens of megabits per second for tens of thousand of users. In an office environment, every node will be offered a capacity of one gigabit per second.
- Very low latencies, enabling real-time interactive applications.

Regardless of how the 5G initiatives turn out in practice, it is safe to assume that mobile networks will evolve quickly, and many more devices will be connected directly to the Internet.

Let's look at what some industry giants have to say:

- We begin with Ericsson, a leading Swedish provider of mobile network hardware. The following is a quote from Ericsson's IoT website:

    "**Ericsson and the Internet of Things**

    More than 40 percent of global mobile traffic runs on Ericsson networks. We are one of the industry's most innovative companies with over 35,000 granted patents, and we are driving the evolution of the IoT by lowering thresholds for businesses to create new solutions powered by modern communications technology; by breaking barriers between industries; and by connecting companies, people and society. Going forward, we see two major opportunity areas:

    Transforming industries: *The IoT is becoming a key factor in one sector after another, enabling new types of services and applications, altering business models and creating new marketplaces.*

    Evolving operator roles: *In the new IoT paradigm, we see three different viable roles that operators can take. An operator's choice on which roles to pursue will depend on factors like history, ambition, market preconditions and their future outlook.*"

Ericsson also contributed to a nice visual dictionary of IoT concepts, which they refer to as the "comic book":

```
http://www.alexandra.dk/uk/services/Publications/Documents/
IoT_Comic_Book.pdf
```

- The networking giant Cisco estimates that the Internet of Things will consist of 50 billion devices connected to the Internet by 2020.

  Cisco prefer to use the term "Internet of Everything" rather than Internet of Things. The company envisions many interesting applications not previously mentioned here. Some of these are:

  - Smart trash bins, where embedded sensors allow the remote sensing of how full a bin is. The logistics of waste management can then be improved.
  - Parking meters that change rates based on the demand.
  - Clothes that notify the user if he or she gets sick.

  All of these systems can be connected and managed together.

- IBM estimate, somewhat more conservatively perhaps, 26 billion devices connected to the Internet by 2020. They provide some examples of applications that are already deployed or in the works:

  - Improved logistics at car manufacturers' using wide sensor net deployments
  - Smarter logistics in health care situations in hospitals
  - Again, smarter logistics and more accurate predictions regarding train travel

Different market players have slightly different predictions for the coming years. At any rate, it seems clear that the Internet of Things will grow nearly exponentially in the coming years. Many new and exciting applications and opportunities will present themselves. It's clear that many fields will be affected by this growth, including, naturally, the field of DevOps.

Machine-to-machine communication

Many of the IoT devices will primarily connect to other machines. As a scale comparison, let's assume every human has a smartphone. That's about 5 billion devices. The IoT will eventually contain at least 10 times more devices—50 billion devices. When this will happen differs a bit among the predictions, but we will get there in the end.

One of the driving forces of this growth is machine-to-machine communication.

Factories are already moving to a greater degree of automation, and this tendency will only grow as more and more options become available. Logistics inside factories can increase greatly with wide sensor net deployments and big data analytics for continuously improving processes.

Modern cars use processors for nearly every possible function, from lights and dashboard functions to window lifts. The next step will be connecting cars to the Internet and, eventually, self-driving cars that will communicate all sensor data to centralized coordinating servers.

Many forms of travel can benefit from the IoT.

IoT deployment affects software architecture

An IoT network consists of many devices, which might not be at the same firmware revision. Upgrades might be spread out in time because the hardware might not be physically available and so on. This makes compatibility at the interface level important. Since small networked sensors might be memory and processor constrained, versioned binary protocols or simple REST protocols may be preferred. Versioned protocols are also useful in order to allow things with different hardware revisions to communicate at different versioned end points.

Massive sensor deployments can benefit from less talkative protocols and layered message queuing architectures to handle events asynchronously.

IoT deployment security

Security is a difficult subject, and having lots of devices that are Internet-connected rather that on a private network does not make the situation easier. Many consumer hardware devices, such as routers, have interfaces that are intended to be used for upgrades but are also easy to exploit for crackers. A legitimate service facility thus becomes a backdoor. Increasing the available surface increases the number of potential attack vectors.

Perhaps you recognize some of these anti-patterns from development:

- A developer leaves a way in the code to enable him or her to later submit code that will be evaluated in the server application context. The idea is that you as a developer don't really know what kind of hot fixes will be necessary and whether an operator will be available when the fix needs to be deployed. So why not leave a "backdoor" in the code so that we can deploy code directly if needed? There are many problems here, of course. The developers don't feel that the usual agreed-upon deployment process is efficient enough, and as an end result, crackers could probably easily figure out how to use the backdoor as well. This anti-pattern is more common than one might think, and the only real remedy is code review.

  Leaving open doors for crackers is never good, and you can imagine the calamity if it was possible to exploit a backdoor in a self-driving car or a heat plant, for instance.

- Unintended exploits, such as SQL injection, mostly occur because developers might not be aware of the problem.

  The remedy is having knowledge about the issue and coding in such a way as to avoid the problem.

Okay, but what about DevOps and the IoT again?

Let's take a step back. So far, we have discussed the basics of the Internet of Things, which is basically our ordinary Internet but with many more nodes than what we might normally consider possible. We have also seen that in the next couple of years, the number of devices with Internet capability in some form or another will keep on growing exponentially. Much of this growth will be in the machine-to-machine parts of the Internet.

But is DevOps, with its focus on fast deliveries, really the right fit for large networks of critical embedded devices?

The classic counterexamples would be DevOps in a nuclear facility or in medical equipment such as pacemakers. But just making faster releases isn't the core idea of DevOps. It's to make faster, more correct releases by bringing people working with different disciplines closer together.

This means bringing production-like testing environments closer to the developers and the people working with them closer together as well.

Described like this, it really does seem like DevOps can be of use for traditionally conservative industries.

The challenges shouldn't be underestimated though:

- The life cycles of embedded hardware devices can be longer than those of traditional client-server computers. Consumers can't be expected to upgrade during every product cycle. Likewise, industrial equipment might be deployed in places that make them expensive to change.

- There are more modes of failure for IoT devices than desktop computers. This makes testing harder.

- In industrial and corporate sectors, traceability and auditability are important. This is the same as for deployments on servers, for instance, but there are many more IoT endpoints than there are servers.

- In traditional DevOps, we can work with small changesets and deploy them to a subset of our users. If the change somehow doesn't work, we can make a fix and redeploy. If a web page renders badly for a known subset of our users and can be fixed quickly, there is only a small potential risk involved. On the other hand, if even a single IoT device controlling something such as a door or an industrial robot fails, the consequences can be devastating.

There are great challenges for DevOps in the IoT field, but the alternatives aren't necessarily better. DevOps is also a toolbox, and you always need to think about whether the tool you pick out of the box really is the right one for the job at hand.

We can still use many of the tools in the DevOps toolbox; we just need to make sure we are doing the right thing and not just implementing ideas without understanding them.

Here are some suggestions:

- Failures and fast turnarounds are okay as long as you are in your testing lab
- Make sure your testing lab is production-like
- Don't just have the latest versions in your lab; accommodate older versions as well

A hands-on lab with an IoT device for DevOps

So far, we have mostly discussed in the abstract sense about DevOps and the IoT and the future of the IoT.

To get a feel for what we can do in hands-on terms, let's make a simple IoT device that connects to a Jenkins server and presents a build status display. This way, we get to try out an IoT device and combine it with our DevOps focus!

The status display will just present a blinking LED in the event that a build fails. The project is simple but can be expanded upon by the creative reader. The IoT device selected for this exercise is quite versatile and can do much more than make an LED blink!

The project will help to illustrate some of the possibilities as well as challenges of the Internet of Things.

The **NodeMCU Amica** is a small programmable device based on the ESP8266 chip from Espressif. Apart from the base ESP8266 chip, the Amica board has added features that make development easier.

Here are some of the specifications of the design:

- There is a 32-bit RISC CPU, the Tensilica Xtensa LX106, running at 80 MHZ.
- It has a Wi-Fi chip that will allow it to connect to our network and our Jenkins server.
- The NodeMCU Amica board has a USB socket to program the firmware and connect a power adapter. The ESP8266 chip needs a USB-to-serial adapter to be connected to the USB interface, and this is provided on the NodeMCU board.
- The board has several input/output ports that can be connected to some kind of hardware to visualize the build status. Initially, we will keep it simple and just use the onboard LED that is connected to one of the ports on the device.
- The NodeMCU contains default firmware that allows it to be programmed in the Lua language. Lua is a high-level language that allows for rapid prototyping. Incidentally, it is popular in game programming, which might offer a hint about Lua's efficiency.

- The device is fairly cheap, considering the many features it offers:

There are many options to source the NodeMCU Amica, both from electronics hobbyist stores and Internet resellers.

While the NodeMCU is not difficult to source, the project is fairly simple from a hardware point of view and might also be undertaken with an Arduino or a Raspberry Pi in practice if those devices turn out to be simpler to gain access to.

Here are some hints for getting started with the NodeMCU:

- The NodeMCU contains firmware that provides an interactive Lua interpreter that can be accessed over a serial port. You can develop code directly over the serial line. Install serial communication software on your development machine. There are many options, such as Minicom for Linux and Putty for Windows.
- Use the serial settings 9600 baud, eight bits, no parity, and one stop bit. This is usually abbreviated to 9600 8N1.
- Now that we have a serial terminal connection, connect the NodeMCU to a USB port, switch to the terminal, and verify that you get a prompt in the terminal window.

If you are using Minicom, the window will look like this:

```
verjo@localhost:/home/verjo                                    ×

Arkiv  Redigera  Visa  Sök  Terminal  Hjälp

NodeMCU 0.9.6 build 20150704  powered by Lua 5.1.4
lua: cannot open init.lua
>
```

Before starting with the code, depending on how your particular NodeMCU was set up at the factory, it might be required to burn a firmware image to the device. If you get a prompt in the previous step, you don't need to burn the firmware image. You might then want to do it later if you require more features in your image.

> To burn a new firmware image, if needed, first download it from the firmware source repository releases link. The releases are provided at https://github.com/nodemcu/nodemcu-firmware/releases

Here is an example `wget` command to download the firmware. The released firmware versions are available in integer and float flavor depending on your needs when it comes to mathematical functions. The integer-based firmware versions are normally sufficient for embedded applications:

```
wget https://github.com/nodemcu/nodemcu-firmware/releases/
download/0.9.6-dev_20150704/nodemcu_integer_0.9.6-dev_20150704.bin
```

You can also build the firmware image directly from the sources on GitHub locally on your development machine, or you can use an online build service that builds a firmware for you according to your own specifications.

The online build service is at http://nodemcu-build.com/. It is worth checking out. If nothing else, the build statistics graphs are quite intriguing.

Now that you have acquired a suitable firmware file, you need to install a firmware burning utility so that the firmware image file can be uploaded to the NodeMCU:

```
git clone https://github.com/themadinventor/esptool.git
```

Follow the installation instructions in the repository's README file.

If you'd rather not do the system-wide installation suggested in the README, you can install the pyserial dependency from your distribution and run the utility from the git-clone directory.

Here's an example command to install the pyserial dependency:

```
sudo dnf install pyserial
```

The actual firmware upload command takes a while to complete, but a progress bar is displayed so that you know what is going on.

The following command line is an example of how to upload the 0.9.6 firmware that was current at the time of writing:

```
sudo python ./esptool.py --port /dev/ttyUSB0 write_flash 0x00000 nodemcu_
integer_0.9.6-dev_20150704.bin
```

If you get gibberish on the serial console while connecting the NodeMCU, you might need to provide additional arguments to the firmware burn command:

```
sudo esptool.py --port=/dev/ttyUSB0 write_flash 0x0 nodemcu_
integer_0.9.6-dev_20150704.bin  -fs 32m -fm dio -ff 40m
```

The esptool command also has some other functionalities that can be used to validate the setup:

```
sudo ./esptool.py read_mac
Connecting...
MAC: 18:fe:34:00:d7:21
```

```
sudo ./esptool.py flash_id
Connecting...
Manufacturer: e0
Device: 4016
```

After uploading the firmware, reset the NodeMCU.

At this point, you should have a serial terminal with the NodeMCU greeting prompt. You achieve this state either using the factory-provided NodeMCU firmware or uploading a new firmware version to the device.

Now, let's try some "hello world" style exercises to begin with.

Initially, we will just blink the LED that is connected to the GPIO pin 0 of the NodeMCU Amica board. If you have another type of board, you need to figure out whether it has an LED and to which input/output pin it is connected in case it does. You can, of course, also wire an LED yourself.

 Note that some variants of the board have the LED wired to the GPIO pin 3 rather than pin 0 as is assumed here.

You can either upload the program as a file to your NodeMCU if your terminal software allows it, or you can type in the code directly into the terminal.

 The documentation for the NodeMCU library is available at http://www.nodemcu.com/docs/ and provides many examples of usage of the functions.

You can first try to light the LED:

```
gpio.write(0, gpio.LOW)  -- turn led on
```

Then, turn off the LED using the following:

```
gpio.write(0, gpio.HIGH) -- turn led off
```

Now, you can loop the statements with some delays interspersed:

```
while 1 do                     -- loop forever
    gpio.write(0, gpio.HIGH) -- turn led off
    tmr.delay(1000000)       -- wait one second
    gpio.write(0, gpio.LOW)  -- turn led on
    tmr.delay(1000000)       -- wait one second
end
```

At this point, you should be able to verify a basic working setup. Typing code directly into a terminal is somewhat primitive though.

There are many different development environments for the NodeMCU that improve the development experience.

 I have a penchant for the Emacs editor and have used the NodeMCU Emacs mode. This mode, NodeMCU-mode, can be downloaded from GitHub. Emacs has an inbuilt facility to make serial connections. The reader should, of course, use the environment he or she feels most comfortable with.

We need some additional hints before being able to complete the lab.

To connect to a wireless network, use the following:

```
wifi.setmode(wifi.STATION)
wifi.sta.config("SSID","password")
```

SSID and password need to be replaced with the appropriate strings for your network.

If the NodeMCU connects properly to your wireless network, this command will print the IP address it acquired from the network's dhcpd server:

```
print(wifi.sta.getip())
```

This snippet will connect to the HTTP server at www.nodemcu.com and print a return code:

```
conn=net.createConnection(net.TCP, false)
conn:on("receive", function(conn, pl) print(pl) end)
conn:connect(80,"121.41.33.127")
conn:send("GET / HTTP/1.1\r\nHost: www.nodemcu.com\r\n"
    .."Connection: keep-alive\r\nAccept: */*\r\n\r\n")
```

You might also need a timer function. This example prints hello world every 1000 ms:

```
tmr.alarm(1, 1000, 1, function()
    print("hello world")
end )
```

Here, Lua's functional paradigm shows through since we are declaring an anonymous function and send it as an argument to the timer function. The anonymous function will be called every 1000 milliseconds, which is every second.

To stop the timer, you can type:

```
tmr.stop(1)
```

Now, you should have all the bits and pieces to complete the labs on your own. If you get stuck, you can refer to the code in the book's source code bundle. Happy hacking!

Summary

In this final chapter, we learned about the emerging field of the Internet of Things and how it affects DevOps. Apart from an overview of the IoT, we also made a hardware device that connects to a build server and presents a build status.

The idea of going from the abstract to the concrete with practical examples and then back again to the abstract has been a running theme in this book.

In *Chapter 1, Introduction to DevOps and Continuous Delivery*, we learned about the background of DevOps and its origin in the world of Agile development.

In *Chapter 2, A View from Orbit*, we studied different aspects of a Continuous Delivery pipeline.

Chapter 3, How DevOps Affects Architecture, delved into the field of software architecture and how the ideas of DevOps might affect it.

In *Chapter 4, Everything is Code*, we explored how a development organization can choose to handle its vital asset—source code.

Chapter 5, Building the Code, introduced the concept of build systems, such as Make and Jenkins. We explored their role in a Continuous Delivery pipeline.

After we have built the code, we need to test it. This is essential for executing effective, trouble-free releases. We had a look at some of the testing options available in *Chapter 6, Testing the Code*.

In *Chapter 7, Deploying the Code*, we explored the many options available to finally deploy our built and tested code to servers.

When we have our code running, we need to keep it running. *Chapter 8, Monitoring the Code*, examined the ways in which we can ensure our code is running happily.

Chapter 9, Issue Tracking, dealt with some of the many different issue trackers available that can help us deal with the complexities of keeping track of development flows.

This is the last chapter in this book, and it has been a long journey!

I hope you enjoyed the trip as much as I have, and I wish you success in your further explorations in the vast field of DevOps!

Index

A

Agile development
  cycles 5
alternative build servers 78
Ansible
  about 120
  implementing 120-122
  versus Puppet 127
Apache Commons Logging 153
apache log4net 153
appender, log4j 154
architecture rules
  about 23
  coupling 24
  principle of cohesion 24
  separation of concerns 23
automated acceptance testing 93-95
automated GUI testing 95
automated integration testing
  about 90
  Arquillian 92
  Docker 91
AWS 132
Azure 132

B

backend integration points
  testing 98, 99
behavior-driven development 93
box 129
branching problem
  defining 45, 46
branching strategy
  selecting 43-45

Bugzilla
  about 168
  bug, creating 171, 172
  bug, resolving 173, 174
  URL 168
  using 170, 171
  workflow 169
build chain 74
build dependencies
  managing 66, 67
build errors
  taking seriously 80
build phases 77, 78
build servers 76
build slaves 72
build status visualization 79
build systems
  faces 62, 63

C

cargo cult Agile fallacy 6, 7
central code repository
  hosting 39
Chef
  about 124
  deploying with 124, 125
client
  selecting 47, 48
client-side logging libraries
  log4j 153
  logback 153
cloud solutions 131
code
  building 61
  defining 41

service interfaces
  maintaining forward compatible 34
shared authentication
  defining 50
Simple Logging Facade for Java (SLF4J) 153
software architecture 21, 22
source code control
  need for 40
source code management
  examples 40
  history 40, 41
source code management system
  migrations, defining 43
  using 42
squashing 55
Subversion 40
SUnit 87
System on a Chip (SoC) 197

T

test automation
  cons 84-86
  pros 84-86
test automation scenario
  about 101
  automated test, running 105
  bug, finding 105
  test walkthrough 105-108
  tricky dependencies, handling
      with Docker 109
  web application, manually testing 102-104
test coverage 89, 90
test-driven development (TDD)
  about 100
  sequence of events 100

three-tier systems
  about 25, 26
  data tier 26
  logic tier 26
  presentation tier 26
Tolerant Reader 34
Trac
  about 174
  URL 174
  using 176-182
triggers 74

U

unit testing
  cons 86

V

Vagrant 128-130
version naming
  defining 46, 47
  principles 46
virtualization stacks 116-118

W

workflow 74, 75
workflows and issues
  examples 161, 162

X

xUnit 87

Thank you for buying
Practical DevOps

About Packt Publishing

Packt, pronounced 'packed', published its first book, *Mastering phpMyAdmin for Effective MySQL Management*, in April 2004, and subsequently continued to specialize in publishing highly focused books on specific technologies and solutions.

Our books and publications share the experiences of your fellow IT professionals in adapting and customizing today's systems, applications, and frameworks. Our solution-based books give you the knowledge and power to customize the software and technologies you're using to get the job done. Packt books are more specific and less general than the IT books you have seen in the past. Our unique business model allows us to bring you more focused information, giving you more of what you need to know, and less of what you don't.

Packt is a modern yet unique publishing company that focuses on producing quality, cutting-edge books for communities of developers, administrators, and newbies alike. For more information, please visit our website at www.packtpub.com.

About Packt Open Source

In 2010, Packt launched two new brands, Packt Open Source and Packt Enterprise, in order to continue its focus on specialization. This book is part of the Packt Open Source brand, home to books published on software built around open source licenses, and offering information to anybody from advanced developers to budding web designers. The Open Source brand also runs Packt's Open Source Royalty Scheme, by which Packt gives a royalty to each open source project about whose software a book is sold.

Writing for Packt

We welcome all inquiries from people who are interested in authoring. Book proposals should be sent to author@packtpub.com. If your book idea is still at an early stage and you would like to discuss it first before writing a formal book proposal, then please contact us; one of our commissioning editors will get in touch with you.

We're not just looking for published authors; if you have strong technical skills but no writing experience, our experienced editors can help you develop a writing career, or simply get some additional reward for your expertise.

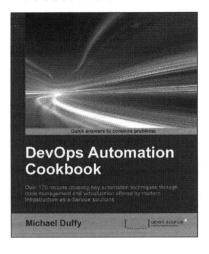

DevOps Automation Cookbook

ISBN: 978-1-78439-282-6   Paperback: 334 pages

Over 120 recipes covering key automation techniques through code management and virtualization offered by modern Infrastructure-as-a-Service solutions

1. Use some of the powerful tools that have emerged to enable systems administrators and developers to take control and automate the management, monitoring, and creation of complex infrastructures.

2. Covers some of the most exciting technologies available to DevOps engineers, and demonstrates multiple techniques for using them.

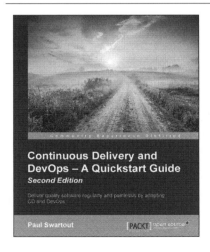

Continuous Delivery and DevOps – A Quickstart Guide

Second Edition

ISBN: 978-1-78439-931-3   Paperback: 196 pages

Deliver quality software regularly and painlessly by adopting CD and DevOps

1. Use DevOps and the Continuous Delivery approach to identify the underlying problems that can stifle the delivery of quality software and overcome them.

2. Learn how Continuous Delivery and DevOps work together with other agile tools.

3. A guide full of illustrations and best practices to help you consistently ship quality software.

Please check **www.PacktPub.com** for information on our titles

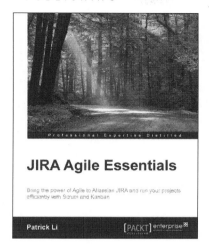

JIRA Agile Essentials

ISBN: 978-1-78439-491-2   Paperback: 132 pages

Bring the power of Agile to Atlassian JIRA and run your projects efficiently with Scrum and Kanban

1. Plan and manage projects effortlessly with JIRA Agile by integrating it with other applications.

2. Improve your team's performance with Scrum and Kanban together with agile methodology.

3. Easy-to-follow learning guide to install JIRA Agile and understand how it fits in with Atlassian JIRA.

The Professional ScrumMaster's Handbook

ISBN: 978-1-84968-802-4   Paperback: 336 pages

A collection of tips, tricks, and war stories to help the professional ScrumMaster break the chains of traditional organization and management

1. Checklists, questions, and exercises to get you thinking (and acting) like a professional ScrumMaster.

2. Presented in a relaxed, jargon-free, personable style.

3. Full of ideas, tips, and anecdotes based on real-world experiences.

Please check **www.PacktPub.com** for information on our titles

Made in the USA
Columbia, SC
15 November 2017